ISBN 978-1-330-27087-5
PIBN 10008328

1 MONTH OF
FREE
READING

at
www.ForgottenBooks.com

English
Français
Deutsche
Italiano
Español
Português

www.forgottenbooks.com

Mythology Photography **Fiction**
Fishing Christianity **Art** Cooking
Essays Buddhism Freemasonry
Medicine **Biology** Music **Ancient**
Egypt Evolution Carpentry Physics
Dance Geology **Mathematics** Fitness
Shakespeare **Folklore** Yoga Marketing
Confidence Immortality Biographies
Poetry **Psychology** Witchcraft
Electronics Chemistry History **Law**
Accounting **Philosophy** Anthropology
Alchemy Drama Quantum Mechanics
Atheism Sexual Health **Ancient History**
Entrepreneurship Languages Sport
Paleontology Needlework Islam
Metaphysics Investment Archaeology
Parenting Statistics Criminology
Motivational

ISLAM,

TURKEY,

AND ARMENIA,

AND

HOW THEY HAPPENED.

""""""""""

By SADIK SHAHID BEY.

TURKISH
MYSTERIES
UNVEILED.

2nd
1898.

PRESS OF
C. B. WOODWARD COMPANY,
ST. LOUIS.

DEDICATION.

This book is gratefully dedicated to my precious mother in far-away Armenia, who possesses my devoted filial love and efforts.

PREFACE.

The frequent requests of many friends, and also realization of the need of a fuller account of the Turkish and Armenian question, have led to the publication of this book.

The object is to understand the life of Mohamet, "The Prophet;" the Koran and its teachings; Islam and its power over Church and State; the Sultan and the Palace; the school and home life of the Turks; also the origin and life of the Armenians, and the causes of the repeated massacres and their results.

The facts given in this book are of the interior of the Empire. Many of the books about Turkey and Armenia are written by men who have made short visits to or lived in the sea-coast cities, writing of what they saw there, which is far from the real Turkish life and practice. The typical Turkish life can not be seen in the sea-coast cities—as Constantinople, Smyrna, Beyrout, Jaffa, etc.—which have slowly lost their originalities through constant contact with Europeans and Americans, who are always present as missionaries and merchants, and visitors in great numbers.

Very few travelers undertake to enter the interior of the Empire. Such parties pass rapidly, and as a rule are guided by Turkish Zabteyahs and are led to the most favorable cities, where the Turkish authorities are prepared to give them a favorable impression. Thus these travelers can know but little about the real situation.

Names of persons and places of events are withheld, lest they cause greater suffering and death to innocent ones.

The attitude of this book toward the Turk is as charitable as the facts could possibly permit.

THE AUTHOR.

EIGHT COMMANDMENTS OF THE KORAN CONCERNING CHRISTIANS.

(THE ARABIC INSCRIPTION ON THE NEXT PAGE.)

(1.) "They are surely infidels, who say, Verily God is Christ the son of Mary." (Koran, Chap. V.)

(2.) "O true believers, take not the Jews or Christians for your friends: they are friends the one to the other; but whoso among you taketh them for his friends, he is surely one of them." (Chap. V.)

(3.) "War is enjoined you against the infidels; but this is hateful unto you; yet perchance ye hate a thing which is better for you, and perchance you love a thing which is worse for you; but God knoweth, and ye know not." (Chap. II.)

(4.) "Fight therefore against them, until there be no temptation to idolatry, and the religion be God's." (Chap. II.)

(5.) "Fight against the friends of Satan, for the stratagem of Satan is weak." (Chap. IV.)

(6.) "And when the months wherein ye are not allowed to attack them shall be past, kill the idolaters wheresoever ye shall find them, and take them prisoners, and besiege them, and lay wait for them in every convenient place." (Chap. IX.)

(7.) "When ye encounter the unbelievers, strike off their heads, until ye have made a great slaughter among them." (Chap. XLVII.)

(8.) "Ye are also forbidden to take to wife free women who are married, except those women whom your right hand shall possess as slaves. This is ordained you from God." (Chap. IV.)

THE ARABIC FORMULA OF THE MOHAMETAN CREED.

"There is no Deity but Allah and
Mohamet is the apostle of Allah."

EIGHT COMMANDMENTS OF THE KORAN CONCERNING THE CHRISTIANS.

(IN ARABIC.)

For the translation see the reverse page.

The diagram of six great massacres of Christians which took place in Turkey within less than seventy-five years.   Every one of these massacres was planned and ordered by the Turkish Government.

1822. Greeks, especially in Scio (Chios) by Sultan Mahmoud, the grandfather of the present Sultan _____50,000

1850. Nestorians and Armenians in Kurdistan, by Sultan Mejit, the father of the present Sultan._____10,000

1860, Maronites and Syrians, in Syria, by the same _____11,000

1876. Bulgarians by Sultan Aziz, the uncle of the present Sultan _____15,000

1894. Armenians at Sassoun, by Sultan Hamid II_____10,000

1895. Armenians, in six provinces, by the same._____90,000

SEVENTY-NINTH PSALM IN ARMENIAN.

(An Armenian mother, writing to her son in the United States, requested him to read the seventy-ninth Psalm in order to know of the situation in Armenia.)

Սաղմոս Ասափայ։

1 Ո՛վ Աստուած՝ հեթանոսները քու ժառան
գութեանդ մէջը մտան․ քուսուրբ տա
ճարդ պղծեցին։ Երուսաղէմը աւերակներու
դարձուցին ։

2 Քու ծառաներուդ դիերը երկինքի թռչուն
ներուն կերակուր տուին , քու սուրբերուդ
մարմինը երկրի գազաններուն ։

3 Անոնց արիւնը Ջուրի պէս Թափեցին Երու
սաղեմին բոլորտիքը , ու մէկը չկար որ զանոնք
Թաղէր ։

4 Մեր դրացիներուն նախատինք եղանք ,
ծաղր ու կատակ մեր բոլորտիքը եղողներուն ։

5 Մինչեւ ե՞րբ՝ ով Տէր․ միշտ պիտի բարկա
նա՞ս․ քու նախանձդ կրակի պէս պիտի բոր
բոքի՞ ։

6 Թափէ՛ քու բարկութիւնդ ան ազգերուն
վրայ՝ որ քեզ չեն ճանչնար , ու ան Թագաւո
րութիւններուն վրայ՝ որ քու անունդ չեն կան
չեր ։

7 Ինչու որ Յակոբը կերան , ու անոր բնակու
թիւնը աւերակ դարձուցին ։

8 Մի յիշեր մեզի դէմ առջի անօրէնութիւն
ները․ Թող շուտով Հասնի մեզի քու ողոր
մութիւններդ․ ինչու որ խիստ Թշուառա
ցանք ։

9 Քու անուանդ փառքին Համար օգնէ՛ մեզի՝
ով մեր փրկութեան Աստուածդ․ եւ քու ա
նուանդ Համար փրկէ՛ մեզ , ու մեր մեղքերը
թափէ՛ ։

10 Ինչու՞ բանն Հեթանոսները , Թէ Ո՞ւր է ա
նոնց Աստուածը․ Թող յայտնուի Հեթանո
սաց մէջ մեր աչքերուն առջեւ քու ծառա
ներուդ Թափուած արիւնին վրէժը ։

11 Կապուածին Հառաչանքը քու առջե՛ւդ Թող
ելլէ․ քու զօրութեանդ մեծութիւնովը մա
հուան մատնուածները ապրեցուր ։

12 Ու եօԹնապատիկ Հատուցում ըրէ մեր դրա
ցիներուն իրենց ծոցին մէջը՝ ան իրենց նախա
տինքին փոխարէն , որով քեզ անարգեցին՝
ով Տէր ։

13 Բայց մենք քու ժողովուրդդ ու քու արօտիդ
ոչխարները յաւիտեան քեզ պիտի գովենք ,
֊֊ քու փառքդ ամէն պատմինք ազգէ մինչեւ
ազգ ։

See also page 222.

CHAPTER I.

MOHAMET, THE FOUNDER OF ISLAM.

1. **The parentage and** traditions about **the** birth of **Mohamet.**—Mohamet was born in Mecca, Arabia, 569 A. D., of a noted parentage belonging to the tribe of Koreish. His father was called Abdullah "the Servant of Allah" (God), and his mother Emineh, "the faithful woman." So remarkable was Abdullah for his personal beauty and other qualities that, according to the Arabic traditions, on the day of his marriage with Emineh 200 virgins of the tribe of Koreish died of broken hearts.

Mohamet was the only child of this most envied family. His birth is related to accompany wonderful events. At the moment of his coming into the world a heavenly light enlightened the surrounding regions, and the new-born babe, raising his eyes to heaven, exclaimed: "Alláhu ékber; la iláhe íllallah, ve énna resúluhu." "Allah is the greatest; there is no deity but Allah, and I am his apostle." In that remarkable night the sacred fire of Zoroaster, which, under the care of Persian magi had burnt without ceasing for more than a thousand years, was said to have been extinguished suddenly, and all the idols in the world and the demons among the stars fell down. The river Tigris bursting its bounds,

11

overflowed the neighboring lands; the palace of the Persian monarch shook to its foundation, several of its towers falling down, and the Judge of Persia saw in his dream a ferocious camel conquered by an Arabian courser.

2. **The Childhood of Mohamet.** His father died either before or shortly after his birth; and the child when two months old was given by his relatives, after the fashion of the land, to a Bedouin nurse to be fostered in genuine desert life. On their journey from the city of Mecca to the tent of the nurse, the tradition says the animal which bore the babe, becoming endowed with speech, proclaimed aloud that it bore on its back the greatest of the Prophets and the favorite of Allah. The flocks of sheep and cattle bowed to him as he passed by, and the moon stooped towards him when he was gazing at it in his cradle.

He could stand alone, the tradition continues to say, when three months old; run abroad when seven; at eight months he could speak so intelligibly and fluently as to astonish all his hearers. At the age of three years, when he was playing in the field with the children of the nurse, two bright angels appeared before them, and taking hold of Mohamet laid him gently upon the ground, and opened his breast without causing any pain, and taking forth his heart washed it with snow from all impurities originated from Adam's sin, and after filling it with faith and wisdom and prophetic light replaced it in his bosom. Mohamet in his later life used to show the crescent-shaped scar of that angelic operation to his followers, who afterwards gave it the title of "the Seal of Prophecy." His nurse and her husband being frightened at this event, which they thought to be an epileptic fit caused by demons, could not dare to keep the child any longer, so took him back to his kindred.

When six years old he lost his mother also, and was adopted by his grandfather, who died in two years, when the child was taken and protected by his uncle. It is supposed that the favorable disposition of the Mohametan law in regard to the widows' and orphans' rights was the result of this early bereavement of his parents and of the experience of an orphan's hard life.

3. The Young Mohamet and his Environment. In the house of his uncle, who was a wealthy merchant, and at the same time the chief guardian of the Kabeh—the most sacred temple of the Arab races from times immemorial—Mohamet was in contact with the commercial and religious leaders. The unceasing arrival and departure of the pilgrims from all parts of the land, and of commercial caravans from the southern and northern districts, caused Mecca to be the seat of a perpetual fair, where, besides the commercial enterprises, the popular traditions of Arabs were recited and various religions were discussed and enforced, and the heroism of the ancient chiefs and the beauty of fair women were sung by celebrated poets, and poetic contests were held before the people, and the poems to which the prize was awarded were re-written in golden characters and suspended in the Kabeh. All these were exciting events for the young Mohamet and carried his

imagination to other parts of the country. At his youthful age and upon his hearty requests his uncle permitted him to accompany some of these caravans in their slow but delightful journeys. The careful observations he made on his way and the interesting tales he heard during his travels, and especially the free and detailed conversations he had with some Nestorian Christian monks residing in a secluded convent, which, being on the way of these caravans, showed great hospitality to them during their journeys from and to home, and other such coincidences, induced the mind of Mohamet to reform the paganish religions of his race by establishing a better system more similar to their original faith supposed to be founded by Abraham and Ishmael, the ancestors of the Arabian races. He was not in favor with the doctrines and practices of Christianity which was divided into various sects, all conflicting with each other and none corresponding with the primitive simplicity of the Apostolic church. He felt much opposition against Judaism of his time and country, calling it a subversion of the ancient religion of Israel, which he mentions very frequently in his later teachings.

4. **The Beginning of the Mohametan Religion.** While forming the design of a new religious system Mohamet was for years in the habit of retiring to a cave not very far from Mecca, and there spending days and weeks in silent meditation. According to some historians his isolation in that cave was not altogether for thoughtful planning, but was due to epileptic fits

to which he was a victim from his childhood. The important crisis having at last arrived—not before his fortieth year, however—he supposed or pretended to have received the first divine communication in the solitude of the cave, where the archangel Gabriel appeared to him in human form, with a written revelation in his hand, which was in Arabic, and giving it to him commanded him to "read." Mohamet, his followers say, did not know how to read, but as soon as he looked over the "waraka" (the writing) he was endowed with a miraculous gift of reading and began to rehearse it fluently and eagerly. This was the first of 114 warakas which Gabriel brought him from time to time and on various occasions, and which, being compiled after the death of Mohamet, composed the book of the Koran.

On the day he received this first divine message he returned home, and at once broke to his wife the solemn news of supernatural visions and heavenly voices in his seclusion, and recited before her the "waraka" which he claimed to be conveyed to him by the archangel Gabriel, and invited her to accept this true religion and to become the first believer among his kindred and countrymen. Being unable to resist such a powerful exhortation, she immediately accepted the invitation and became the first proselyte among the future hosts of the Mohametan world.

5. **The Rapid Progress of Islam.** Mohamet's teachings, especially those that were against the idols of Kabeh, were very much opposed by his own tribe and kindreds. But owing to the circumstances of his

time and country, namely, to the discord and corruption among the Christian sects, and the hostility between the proselyte Jews and the Christians, and to the adaptation of Islamic militio-religious system to the adventurous spirit of the Arab races, and to the sensual and avaricious nature of savage tribes, and to the absence of a mighty power to check its fury, this system was firmly established in Arabia "by the edge of the sword," and these local successes encouraged the followers of Islam to carry on their expeditions by the force and fire of the "Holy Wars" which burned all the surrounding countries, ruined and defiled the Christian churches, killed and enslaved the Jews and the Christians, until, in the short space of 80 years from the death of their prophet they could extend the Mohametan dominion from Egypt to India, and from Lisbon to Samarcand, thus waving the bloody banner of the "Crescent" over the continents of Asia, Africa and Europe. Had it not been for the bravery of Charles Martel Europe would have been overwhelmed by the torrent of Islam, and would most probably be covered with its gloom even unto this day. As an illustration of the rapid progress of Islam, so much would suffice to mention that in the fourth year of his mission Mohamet could only make 40 Proselytes, chiefly slaves and the people of the lower ranks, while towards the twentieth year of his ministry he entered the city of Mecca with 40,000 followers to perform pilgrimage in the Kabeh, the sacred temple that was already Mohametanized. The present number of Mohametans is estimated to be over 200,000,000.

CHAPTER II.

1. **The Asserted Supremacy of the Koran.**
Mohammetans confess four sacred books, Law of
Moses, Psalms of David, Gospel of Jesus and Koran
of Mohamet, with these two distinctions, that the
Koran, being the last and the best of the revelations,
is supreme and authoritative over the others, and
that the present books, which Jews and Christians
have in their hands, are not the genuine revelations
given to Moses, David and Jesus; that the Jewish
and Christian scribes intentionally corrupted them in
order to conceal all indications about the Latter
Day Prophet and his true religion. Hence they
have no value as authoritative texts and no Mohametan need be led astray by them, as the substance of
the original revelations is given in the book of Koran.

The original text of the Koran, they assert,
exists upon a tablet co-existent with the throne of
God and adored by the celestial hosts as "the
Eternal Word." A copy of it, written with silver
and golden letters, descended into the first heaven in
the sacred month of Ramazan, and piece by piece
communicated to Mohamet by the archangel Gabriel.
Each letter of this holy book is said to contain ten
thousand mysteries and unmeasurable virtues.
Simply the heading of each chapter, "Bismilláh er
rahmán errahim" (in the name of the most merciful
Allah), being composed of 19 Arabic letters, is be-

17

lieved to have sufficient power to dispel the evils of
the 19 hours of the day, and united with five
daily Mohametan prayers is able to keep the believer
from the evils and troubles of a whole day. The
mechanical rehearsing of certain passages is taught to
be an effectual relief for certain calamities, a sure
protection in sacred wars, a lucky success in all
enterprises, and an assurance in gaining loves and
favors.

2. **The Sacredness of the Current Copies of the
Koran.** A non-Mohametan is not allowed to touch
this heaven-descended book; even the Mohametans
do not handle it without having first performed the
ceremony of ablution—sacred washing. When
European or American travelers go to the Turkish
Museums at Constantinople and enter, for instance,
into the Tomb of Sultan Mahmoud, they will find a
Mohametan guide there ready to show and explain the
articles of interest, among which are several copies
of the Koran wrapped in elegant embroideries and
put upon special stands in front of the tomb, both
for adornment and for the spiritual benefit of that
great Sultan. The guide opens them one by one
and explains their authority and dates and estimated
prices, always being careful that no infidel's hand
shall touch them. If any of the visitors moves his
hand toward the finely gilded pages he politely pushes
it back, saying, "Please, sir, according to our belief
it is not lawful to touch the sacred Koran without
first performing the legal ceremony of ablution. I
can not myself touch it without." The writer had

the opportunity to examine the very fine pages and richly ornamented covers while the white-turbaned guide was busy in telling stories about the out-of-order "golden clock," which was presented to a previous Sultan by the Emperor Napoleon, and the heavy embroidered green curtains used many years in the "Sacred Kabeh," and forwarded to him as a compliment to his religious zeal; and the chest in which "the sacred beard" of the Prophet is still preserved, which no one is allowed to open but the Sultan himself when he comes to kiss the sacred relics kept in that magnificent shrine of white marbles.

Such a book of boundless mysteries and rich blessings can never be translated into other languages; hence the Arabs, the Hindoos, the Moors, the Persians, the Turks and the Albanians, all different races with different dialects, read it in the same original Arabic language with the strictest care of correct articulation. A great many learned people make it their life work to commit the whole Koran (a book about t e size of the New Testament) to memory and rehearse it continually. Even the majority of the blind men among Mohametans learn the whole book by heart, and on various occasions are invited into the Harems to rehearse certain portions for their own interest and for the benefit of the household. They are called "Hafiz," the Preserver (of the ancient Word).

It is n t an unusual thing to see a pious Mohametan sit before the window of his house, or even at his shòp, and engage in repeating or reading his Koran in a monotonous tone and with continual vibrations of the upper part of his body, at the same time noticing all things about, having occasional talks with others, trying to catch the neighbors' customers, bargaining, joking, swearing, cursing, as the circumstances may demand, and yet trying to finish the portion he began to recite. The great majority can not read the Koran, but they are privileged to carry about them some portions of it written upon a narrow and very long piece of paper, and wrapped in cloth very tightly and put in a tin or silver case and hung around the neck. The simple carrying of such a relic entitles the owner to the same blessings, and he is requested to take it out from time to time—once in a few years, for example—and hand it to a teacher and listen to his reading it. Many children, sleepless babies, idiots and even mad animals are furnished with such relics in order to be protected from "bad eyes" and possible injuries.

3. **Bible Stories as Recorded in the Koran.** By his accidental contact with the Christians and Jews Mohamet seems to have received some vague idea of the Old and New Testaments and the apocryphal and Talmudic writings of his time. The Mohametan so-called Bible story is full of mistakes, as it will be seen from the following examples:

The Story of Adam and Eve. After creating Adam God brought him into the presence of angels and commanded them to bow before this human being [the reason of this command will be given else-

where], which they all have done except Azazil, one
of the four distinguished archangels, who refused,
saying, "Why should I, whom Thou hast created of
fire, bow down to one whom Thou hast formed of
clay?" For this offense and rebellion he was accursed
and cast out of Paradise, and his name changed to
Iblis, which signifies "despair." In revenge for his
abasement he works all kinds of mischief against the
posterity of Adam.

After eating the forbidden fruit, and being expelled from Paradise, which was in heaven, Adam
was cast down to India and Eve to Jiddeh in Arabia,
where they wandered alone 200 years without being
able to find each other. On Adam's lamenting, God
forgave his sin and led him to the districts of Mecca,
where he found his wife, no more to separate. Eve
gave twenty births, two children each time, one male
and the other female. And God commanded each
male to marry his next younger sister. Cain (they
call *Cabil*) being disobedient to this divine order,
wanted to marry the girl who was born with him.
So God being displeased with him, did not accept his
offering as He did that of Abel. Adam lived a
thousand years and saw 40,000 of his descendants,
after which he died on a Friday (the sacred day
of the Mohametans) and was buried in the island of
Serendib, Ceylon.

Seth, the son of Adam, being the most beautiful
among mankind, and a favorite of his father, received
fifty pieces of revelation from God, and also built the
Kabeh with stone and lime.

The Tradition about Kabeh, the Holy Temple in Mecca. Adam one day, in the depth of his sorrow and repentance, raised his hands and eyes to heaven and implored the kindness of God that a shrine might be granted to him similar to that which he had worshiped while in Paradise, and around which the angels used to move in adoring processions. The prayer of Adam was heard and a tabernacle formed of radiant clouds which was lowered down by the angels. Toward this shrine Adam thenceforth turned when in prayer, and around it he daily made seven circuits in imitation of the angelic procession. At the death of Adam it passed away or was drawn up to heaven, but another of the same form and on the same spot was built of stone and clay by Seth. This was swept away by the deluge.

After many generations, when Hagar and her child, Ishmael, were near perishing from thirst in the desert, an angel revealed to them a spring of water near the ancient site of that tabernacle. This spring or well, called Zemzem, is held sacred by the descendants of Ishmael to the present day. In process of time, by the command of God, Ishmael undertook to rebuild the Kabeh, assisted by his father, Abraham. While they were thus occupied the angel Gabriel brought them a stone which was originally the guardian angel appointed to watch over Adam in Paradise, but changed into a stone and thrown out with him as a punishment for not being more watchful. This stone Abraham and Ishmael received with proper reverence and put it in a corner of the exterior wall of the temple, where it remains to the present day, devoutly kissed by worshipers each time they make a circuit around the building.   When first inserted in the wall it was a single jacinth of dazzling whiteness, but became gradually blackened by the kisses of sinful mortals.   At the resurrection day it will recover its angelic form and stand forth a testimony before God in favor of those who have performed the holy pilgrimage.

The Story of the Prophets and Abraham.   Mohametans accept 200,000 prophets or holy men, 313 of whom, being endowed by special pieces of divine revelation, are called the apostles or the messengers. Six of this latter class, Adam, Noah, Abraham, Moses, Jesus and Mohamet, had preference over all by special mission to establish new religious systems among mankind.

Mohamet being the last and the greatest of this group of six is called "The Prophet of the Latter Days," "The Favorite of God," "The Glory of the Universe," "The Prince of Two Worlds," "The Seal of the Prophets," "The Unique Pearl," "The Chief of the Apostles," etc.

Next in excellence comes Abraham, "Halil Ullah," the Friend of God, upon whose faith, they say, the religion of Islam was founded.   They give preference to Ishmael, the patriarch of Arabs, over Isaac, the patriarch of Jews.   Among the many Arabic traditions of Abraham the following is selected to be the fact related in the Koran: Abraham, a worshiper of the Almighty, was persecuted by his tribe and by his own family. One day the infidel king of his country, hearing about the heresy of young Abraham, summoued him into his presence and commanded him to give up the worship of God and worship the statue of his king, who was greater than God. Abraham not obeying his command was cast into a furnace of fire, which by the divine power was immediately changed to a shining glory. Seeing this miraculous heavenly light many unbelievers turned to God, but the haughty ruler was still more obstinate and insisted upon his supremacy over all gods. One day in a dispute Abraham said unto him, "Verily my God bringeth the sun from the east, now do thou bring it from the west if thou art equal to God." Upon this challenge the infidel was confounded and ordered Abraham out of his dominion. As soon as Abraham left the city a mighty wind was sent by God and destroyed it even to its foundations. When Abraham saw the city in this condition he deplored and thought in his heart, how shall God quicken this city. Then God caused him to die for a hundred years and afterwards raised him to life and said unto him, "How long hast thou tarried here?" He answered, "A day, or part of it." God said, "Nay, thou hast tarried here a hundred years; now look on thy food and drink, they are not yet corrupted; but look on thine animal, which is long dead and the bones scattered. See how I will raise them and clothe them with flesh." And He did according to His word. Then in order to make the doctrine of resurrection plainer to him he told Abraham to take four birds and divide them into pieces, and lay a part of them on every mountain and then call them together, which he did, and the birds being restored to life came swiftly unto him.

The Story of Jesus Christ. Mohametans regard "Isa el Messih," Jesus, the Christ, with high reverence, and attribute his miraculous birth to the power of God, but condemn the Christians with utmost severity for calling him "God," or "the Son of God." Among the thousand and one Arabic names of divinity they never accept the title of "Father."

The outline of his life as taken from the Koran is as follows: Mary retired from her family to a place towards the east, and took a veil to conceal herself from men. One day the angel Gabriel appeared unto her and said, " Verily I am the messenger of thy Lord, and sent to give thee a holy son for a sign unto men." Wherefore she conceived and retired aside to a more distant place. And when the pains of childbirth came upon her she reclined upon the trunk of a palm tree and cried, saying, "Would to God I had died before this and lost in oblivion!" When the child came she took him in her arms and brought to her people, who being unaware of all these things, with great contempt said unto her, "O Mary, sister of Aaron, now thou hast done a strange thing; thy father was not a bad man, neither was thy mother a harlot!" But she made signs unto the new-born child to answer them and tell the truth all about himself, whereupon he said "Verily I am the servant of God, he hath given me the book of the gospel and hath appointed me a

prophet, and hath commanded me to observe prayer
and to give alms so long as I shall live. Peace be on
me the day whereon I was born and the day whereon
I shall die and the day whereon I shall be raised to
life." When Jesus was grown enough to begin his
prophecy he took clay from earth and made it in the
figure of a bird, and breathing thereon it became a
living bird by God's permission. On another occasion
he caused a table to descend unto his apostles from
heaven, and the day of its descent became a festival
day unto Christians. In one of his discourses Jesus
is related to speak unto his followers that in latter
days there will arise a greater prophet called
"Ahmed," glorious (another title of Mohamet),
and the world shall obey him. Mohametans assert
that the Jewish and Christian scribes maliciously
corrupted the books of law and gospel and took out
the name of Mohamet from the original writings.

They never believe that Jesus was actually held,
crucified and murdered by the Jews, but simply they
were deceived by a divine trick in taking Simon,
the betrayer, for Jesus, because God has given him
the resemblance of his master in order to punish him
for his treason, and to annul the bad intention of the
enemies while he took Jesus into heaven, whence he
shall come in the last day to testify for Mohamet.
In that day God shall say unto Jesus before all
Christians, "O Jesus, son of Mary, hast thou said
unto men to take thee and thy mother for two gods
beside God?" He shall answer solemnly, "Praise be
unto Thee! It is not for me to say that which I

ought not; thou knowest what is in me. I have not spoken to them any other than what thou didst command me."

These few illustrations of the so-called Mohametan bible story will be enough to show that the illiterate founder of that false religion, partly misled, of course, by the apocryphal Christian writings of his age, tried to conceal his fraud by childish stories, by unnecessary details and wholly false representations, at the same time making gross mistakes in geographical and historical facts; e. g., he makes the prophet Elijah contemporary with Moses; Ishmael to have been offered in sacrifice instead of Isaac; Saul to have led the ten thousand down to the river bank instead of Gideon, and by the most monstrous error represents Mary, the mother of Jesus, to have been the same person with Miriam, the sister of Aaron and Moses!

4. **A Few Quotations from the Koran.** In order to get a clearer idea about the moral character of this sacred book let us read some pieces from it. The first chapter reads as follows: "In the name of the most merciful Allah. Praise be to Allah, the Lord of all creatures, the most gracious, the king of the day of judgment. Thee do we worship, and of thee do we beg assistance. Direct us in the right way, in the way of those to whom thou hast been gracious; not of those against whom thou art incensed, nor those who go astray." For the sake of impartiality we have quoted one of the *best* portions, which any Mohametan himself would bring in favor

of the Koran; but before giving any decision let us read some other portions, as

From the 2nd Chapter. "When the Lord said unto the angels, 'I will place a substitute on earth' (he referred to Adam), they said, 'Wilt thou place there one who will do evil therein and shed blood? but we celebrate thy praise and sanctify Thee.' God answered, 'Verily I know that which ye know not;' and he taught Adam the names of all things, and then proposed them to the angels and said, 'Declare unto me now the names of these things if ye say truth.' They answered, 'Praise be unto thee, we have no knowledge but what thou teachest us, for thou art knowing and wise.' God said, 'O Adam, tell them now their names;' and when he had told them their names, God said, 'Did I not tell you that I know the secrets of heaven and earth?' and when he said unto the angels, 'Now worship Adam,' they all worshiped him except Iblis, who refused and was puffed up with pride, and became of the number of unbelievers," etc. This is an example of illogical and objectionable stories with which "the Ancient Word" is full. God's resentful consultation with the angels, their knowledge about the future condition of mankind and at the same time their ignorance in telling the names of things; God's fraud in teaching Adam secretly, yet in showing the angels that he (Adam) knew the names himself, and thus gaining a false name for Adam, whom he decided to appoint a substitute in spite of the angels. These are some of the contradictions and blasphemous points.

Another example from the 56th Chapter. "Those who have preceded others in the faith shall precede them to paradise. These are they who shall approach near unto God; they shall dwell in gardens of delight, reposing on couches adorned with gold and precious stones, sitting opposite to one another thereon. Youth, which shall continue in their bloom forever, shall go round about to attend them with goblets and beakers and a cup of flowing wine; their head shall not ache by drinking the same, neither shall their reason be disturbed; and with fruits of the sorts which they shall choose, and the flesh of birds of the kind which they shall desire. And there shall accompany them fair damsels having large black eyes, resembling pearls hidden in their shells, as a reward for that which they shall have wrought. Verily we have created the damsels of Paradise by a peculiar creation, and we (God is the speaker) have made them virgins, beloved by their husbands, of equal age with them, for the delight of the companions of the right hand," etc. This is the sketch of the description of Mohametan Paradise, with which the sacred Koran is full.

5. **Koran's Declaration and Commands about Christians.** "They are surely infidels who say, Verily God is Christ, the son of Mary" (*Chap. 4*). "O true believers, take not the Jews or Christians for your friends, they are friends the one to the other; but whoso among you taketh them for his friends he is surely one of them" (*Chap. 5*).

"War is enjoined you against *the infidels*, but this is hateful unto you; but God knoweth and ye know not." "Fight, therefore, against them until there be no temptation to delusion and the religion to God's" (*Chap. 2*). "And when the (sacred) months, wherein ye are not allowed to attack them, shall be passed, kill the associates (of divinity, polytheists and trinitarians) wheresoever ye shall find them and take them prisoners, and besiege them, and lay wait for them in every convenient place" (*Chap. 9*). " When ye encounter the unbelievers, strike off their heads until ye have made a great slaughter among them" (*Chap. 47*). "Let them fight for the religion of God, who part with the present life in exchange for that which is to come; for whosoever fighteth for the religion of God, whether he be slain or be victorious, we will surely give him a great reward" (*Chap. 4*). "Fight against them who profess not the true religion, of those unto whom the scriptures have been delivered (Jews and Christians) until they pay tribute by right of subjection, and they be reduced low" (*Chap. 9*). "Ye are also forbidden to take to wife free women who are married, except those women whom your right hand shall possess as slaves. This is ordained you from God" (*Chap. 4.*)

The above precepts are a few examples of the diabolic spirit of Islam, with which the whole Koran is saturated. And the most blasphemous side of this is that these words profess to be copied from the "Eternal Word of God," and descended from heaven and from the mouth of the just and merciful God.

CHAPTER III.

According to the doctrines and practice of Islam non-Mohametans have no right to enjoy the same privileges God has granted to Moslems. They may be allowed to live among Moslems only as subjects and subordinates, in a very restricted limitation in regard to their legal rights, religious privileges and titles of honor and social freedom.

1. Titles Denied in the Koran to non-Mohametans. The Mohametans call themselves "Muslim" (Moslem) which signifies "Submitted" to Allah and his service body and soul, and destined to peace and salvation. Also "Mumin," the "Believer" of the true God and his angels and holy servants. Also "Ibadullah," the servants and worshipers of Allah. Again, "Ummeti Muhammed," the people or the flock of Mohamet, etc. The followers of any other religion, idolators, atheists, Sabians, magi, Jews and Christians, are called "Kiafir" (Giaour), blasphemer, infidel.

Sultan Mahmoud II., the grandfather of the present Sultan, has formally forbidden his subjects to apply the term Giaour to any European, and one or two of his successors extended this prohibition to the Christian and Jewish subjects of their own dominions; but such things being well known to be insincere could not and did not bring any change. The followers of the false prophet practice the same insulting titles now and will continue to do so as long as Islam rules.

How can the Mohametans honor Christians whom the Koran declares as "those who go astray," "unbelievers," "polytheists," "corrupt doers," "fools," "despised," "hypocrites," etc. etc.? These are the names given to non-Mohametans in the book of Koran, "the latest and best of Divine revelations," in which nothing is more prevalent than the contrast of Moslems' and non-Moslems' present and future conditions. The idea of universal brotherhood of mankind and the attempt to promote the final union of the Kingdom of God are the points most maliciously ignored in its pages."

2. **Other Popular Titles of Disgrace Used for non-Mohametans.** The mosques of Moslems are called "Jami Sherif," the sacred convent; to the word "kiliseh," church, they never attach the adjective *sacred*. The metropolitan mosques or temples are called "Beitullah or Seiretullah," the house of God or the walking place of God, while the Christian cathedrals are called "Ulu Kilisch," the big gathering place. The common, rude Mohametan chapels, most of which are not worthy for human habitation, are named "Mesjid" (mosque), the worshiping place, while Christian chapels are named "gathering place." The graves of distinguished Mohametans are called "Turbet Sherif," the sacred tomb, while those of Christians

"Makbereh," the burial place. The religious services of Islam are called "sejdeh, or ibadet," worship or service of God, while those of non-Moslems, "rites, forms, ceremonies." The supposed mantle of Mohamet, kept with greatest care and honor, is called "Hurkai Sherif," the sacred mantle, but the cross sign of the Christians' "Salab," the hanging wood. The religious chief of Islam is titled "Emir el Mumin," the sire, the commander of the believers. The Christian patriachs, or archbishops, are called "Patrik or Serpiscopos; "Ser" means head, "Pis" means filth—"Filthy-headed Copos." The bishops are popularly called "Karabash," the black-headed; the common priests, "Keshish," which has no literal meaning. The Jewish high priest is called "Khakham Bashi," the Boss Khakham (corrupted from the Hebrew word "Hakem," the sage). The Mohametan theological teachers are called "Muderris," explainer, interpreter; that of the Christians (vartabed) "Mahrasah"—mashed food, hash. A Mohametan pilgrim to Mecca is called "Haji"— holy pilgrim. A Christian pilgrim to Jerusalem "Aji"—the bitter one. The noted men among the Mohametans are called "Effendi, agha," sire, yeoman; among the Christians, "Chorbaji," soup-maker. The learned Mohametans, "Khoja," master; Christians, "Havaja," airy, nonsense, fool. The Moslem women, "Haremi Sherif, Cadin," the sacred harem, the lady; the Christian women, "Giaour Mamasi," the infidel old woman, the mother of infidels. Their Friday is called "Aziz

Juma," the holy convention. Our Sunday is called "Ahad," the first day of the week, or "Bazar," the sale day. The Mohametan fasting month is called "Ramazani Sherif," the sacred Ramazan; the Christian Lent is called "Behriz," the corruption of "Perhiz," abstinence from certain foods. The Mohametan dead is called "Jenazeh," the funeral worship; that of a Christian is called "Giaour olusi," the dead body of an infidel. When they announce in the papers the death of a noted Moslem they say, "Transferred into the Land of Perpetuity," or "Migrated into the Region of Souls;" of any Christian they say "shriveled, perished." When they mention a dead Mohametan they say, "May God have mercy unto his soul," or "May his tomb be illuminated," or "Peace be upon him." They never use such phrases for the Christians. Of the former sultans they say, "Whose abode is Paradise."

3. **Christians Disgraced in Official Documents.** In a Turkish dictionary, published at Constantinople not very long ago, the word "jeres" (bell) is defined as "the special instrument by which the Blasphemers call their people to perform heathenish rites," and this was fifty years later than the formal prohibition of the Sultan Mahmoud II., "whose abode is Paradise."

It was custom until very recent times to attach the title of "Zimmi," indebted, to any Christian name in writings, because, according to the declaration of the Koran. Christians are indebted to the Moslem's mercy for their existence and some privileges (for which they have to pay tribute as a ransom fee); also the Christians are called "Rayah," *pasture*, for the flock of Moslem lambs.

They write "Ahmed, the son of Mohamet," to identify a Moslem, but "Peter, born of John," for Christians. This is simply to denounce Christian marriage as illegal. When mixed names are to be put on paper the eminent Christian's name must come after the name of a common Moslem's, the distinction of adjectives never being omitted.

The following official document of a certain Mah-kemeh, legal court, given not very long ago in con-nection with the burial of a Christian priest, is among the properties of the said person, and reads as follows:

"From the estrayed sect of Nazarites the infidel Keshish, named—having been shriveled (dead), the official permission of our sacred Mahkemeh was im-plored by his sect to put the corpse under the earth. Though the accursed carrion of the said wretch is not worthy to be placed under the sacred soil, which will refuse the admission of such an unclean thing, yet in order to prevent the stench of atmosphere by the hateful stink of the perished body, this official docu-ment is written and given as a permission for taking away the said filth to their assigned spot, and put it under the soil according to their vain ceremonies. May it stumble down to the infernal abyss."

The grave-stone of Christians is not allowed to stand erect, but must be prone, in token of their sub-jection to Mohametan rule.

4. Denial of Religious and Social Rights. According to the Mohametan law a non-Moslem's testimony cannot be accepted, even listened to, in legal courts, especially when it tends to be against a "believer." But when the interest of Islam demands, a Moslem is justified, even held religiously obliged, to go to the court and give his legal oath and bear false witness against Giaours (Christians.) This is sanctioned by a decree of the Koran and practiced by its followers.

A Christian can never make a legal will on his own property, leaving it for his church, or school, or any Christian institution; while most of the wealthy Mohametans will their immovable properties to a certain mosque, or even to their living generations or friends, and such properties, by a very small religious fee, are forever exempt from the regular taxation, regarded as the sacred possession of Islam, carefully protected, repaired, and prevented from being sold to others, especially to "Giaours."

A Christian church, or school, or any other public institution cannot be erected within sixty yards distance from a mosque or Moslem school, even if the latter be ruined and changed to a heap of ashes.

The words of common salutation used among Moslems, "Peace be unto you," can never be addressed to or by a Christian, because this phrase being used among the ancient Moslem prophets, as Adam, Noah, Abraham, Moses, David, Jesus and others, and also among the angels and saints of Paradise, no infidel destined to perdition has a right to claim its benefit.

If addressed to a Christian by mistake it must be and is withdrawn at once. When they meet a Christian acquaintance they *may* use common words of recognition or make a slight motion with their hand without uttering a word.

5. **Practical Enmity Against Christianity.** No Moslem can change his faith without infliction of the death penalty. Especially those who are proselyted to Islam can never return to their original faith without being murdered for the supposed treason, while Christian men and women are induced, forced, and very often tortured to accept Islam. To marry such a convert woman is regarded highly virtuous. In case of such a conversion, which *is very rare*, the once Christian man is clothed with a heavily embroidered robe and a rich turban put upon his head, and mounted upon a fine horse and accompanied with a crowd of howling dervishes and singing mollahs he is paraded in the streets and by the houses of his former friends; then he is taken to the house of the greatest Moslem and entertained there for several days until a believing woman is found to marry this new-born servant of Allah, who with his faith changes also his name.

Such common proverbs are publicly spoken, even to the face of the Christians: "Giaour's property is lawful to Moslem;" "Giaour's neck is for the sword of Islam;" "Giaour's head belongs to the government, and his property to the public;" "It is virtuous to drink Giaour's blood;" "Giaour has no religion;" "On the Day of Resurrection Giaours shall grovel with their faces on the earth, while the Moslems will walk erect, and will be borne aloft on winged camels, white as milk, with saddles of fine gold;" "When the Bridge of Surat is reached the Moslem will pass it through as a bird or an arrow and step the blissful gardens of Paradise, but Giaours, finding it as narrow as a hair's breadth and as sharp as a sword, will not be able to walk upon it, and thus shall stumble down into the lake of hell, full of boiling slime and melted sulphur;" "If a man kills an innocent cat or dog he must build as many mosques as the number of hairs on the animal, in order to escape its future punishment, but by killing obstinate Jews or Christians will be rewarded in both worlds."

Every pious Moslem has to repeat the following prayer when he kneels down before the throne of his most merciful Allah: "I seek refuge with Allah from Satan, the accursed; in the name of Allah, the most merciful. O Lord of all creatures, O Allah! destroy the infidels and polytheists, Thine enemies, the enemies of *the* religion. O Allah! make their children orphans, and defile their abodes; cause their feet to slip; give them and their families, their households and their women, their children and their relatives by marriage, their brothers and their friends, their possessions and their race, their wealth and their lands, as booty to the Moslems. O Lord of all creatures!"

CHAPTER IV.

THE FIVE RELIGIOUS DUTIES OF ISLAM.

1. **Prayer.** Mohametans have five daily prayers, which are nothing but mechanical repetition of some portions from the religious books, in appointed times and in certain manner.

At first Allah demanded forty daily prayers from the Moslems, but through the intercession and wise counsel of the Greatest Prophet, he was willing to reduce the number to five. The time for first prayer is at one hour before sunrise, the second at noon, the third two hours before sunset, the fourth at sunset, and the last about two hours after sunset.

Prayers must be preceded by ablution, the ceremonious washing of the hands, arms, nostrils, mouth, face, ears, forehead and feet.

Each time of prayer a crier called "muezzin" ascends to the top of the minaret, the slim, high tower attached to the mosque, to invite the believers to worship. He must cry as eagerly and loudly as he can, by which he will be able to reach more people, and also secure a larger space in paradise, as large as the distance of his voice.

To pray with the congregation is regarded more virtuous, but in case of necessity the believer may perform his prayer at home, in the shop, in any public place, or on the wayside. The Friday noon prayer, the evening prayers of the fasting month and the morning prayers of the Great Festival days are expected to be performed in the mosque.

At prayer Kabeh, the sacred temple of Mcca, must be faced. If a traveler confuses the directions he may face any direction by uttering ''My intention is the Kabeh.'' Shoes must be taken off, but hats kept on. The various positions during the worship are standing erect, the eyes fixed low upon the ground, then partial bending of the body and kneeling, then touching the floor with the forehead, which is repeated several times. While in these attitudes the worshiper will repeat certain passages from the Koran in a low, muttering way. The very act of looking around, talking, laughing, coughing, spitting, sneezing, or rubbing the flesh in consequence of a fly-bite, renders the unfinished prayer null and void and obliges the worshiper to begin his devotion anew.

The Mohametans never pray in a place where any picture may be found. You can not see pictures or photographs in Moslem houses, except in those of a very few liberal minded officers. Mohamet used to say that ''the angels would not enter a house in which pictures are found, and that those who made them would be commanded in the last day to give souls to them, or be punished in the fire of hell.'' Some carry this piety to the degree that they scratch the necks of the pictures on foreign coins with a knife, as if to kill or nullify them. There are Napoleons, Victorias, czars, kaisers and Austrian emperors—all *intimate friends* of the Sultan and *protectors* of his throne—that circulate with *scratched necks* in Moslem markets, especially in the interior of the Ottoman empire, where the actual scratch-necks has been so freely going on by the order of "the most gracious father of the empire," and before the eyes of his great allies.

2. **Fasting During the Month of Ramazan** (lunar calendar). During the twenty-nine days of this month all the adult Moslems must fast from dawn to sunset, after which they are let loose to eat and drink and smoke and do all kinds of carnal deeds all the night. The sick and the travelers are allowed to omit this duty upon the condition that they perform it at another convenient time. Any man who fails to keep the fast is disgraced and punished publicly, occasionally by being seized and put on a donkey seated backwards and the tail in his hand for the bridle, and carried all over the market places, followed by a shouting multitude. Sometimes as an additional attraction to this religio-maniacal parade the face of the person is dyed black.

In this sacred month of prayer and humiliation their religious feelings—namely, their carnal desires, their laziness and their enmity and brutality against Giaours—reach to the highest pitch. Poor Christians suffer more in this single month than in the other eleven months. Every Christian must be very cautious not to excite the "long-faced" Moslem by demanding his debt, or by eating or smoking in his presence, or by disturbing his ear with songs or church bells.

Ramazan is believed to be the month in which the
Koran descended from the seventh to the first heaven,
and in which Mohamet had a night's journey to
heaven. In the fourteenth night of that month
the archangel Gabriel aroused him by gently touching his side and led him out of his house, where a
winged mule waited for them. They both rode the
animal, which took them in a moment to the top of
Mount Sinai; the next moment they were in the
Temple of Jerusalem, at the gate of which they left
the mule, and Gabriel, carrying Mohamet upon his
wings, put him on the threshold of heaven. After
visiting all the seven stages of heaven he approached to the throne of the Almighty and saw the
eternal plate upon which "the Word of Ages" was
written. Mohamet testifies that upon each gate of
heaven he saw the Arabic inscription, "There is no
deity but Allah, and Mohamet is the Apostle of
Allah." After this miraculous visit and glorious
vision he was taken home by the same route. In
this illustrious night, "El Kadr," there was an extraor-
dinary calmness on the earth, so that the roaring
streams kept still, the winds did not blow, the poison-
ous serpents and the ferocious animals were motion-
less in their dens, the robbers could not go out to
their business, and the diseases and the evil spirits
were controlled.

3. **Pilgrimage to the Sacred Kabeh at Mecca.**
This is a duty put upon those who can afford the expenses and bear the troubles of the long and tiresome
journey. If one can not go himself he may send a

substitute, the virtue being the same. The day when the sacred caravans start towards the holy city of Mecca is regarded as a great occasion, both for those who will make the pilgrimage and those who are sending them. Almost all the Moslem population of the town or city are gathered in one place, dervishes with their drums and holy banners, large turbaned and wide-robed mollahs, with their yellow slippers, followed by a great multitude of men, women and children, some howling and singing, others talking and crying, some swearing, others trading, all on foot, forming a scene of Babylonian confusion and Sodomite rage. The chief motive of this tumult is two-fold: one is to make a great religious demonstration against the Christians, and the other for their belief that every Moslem who accompanies the sacred caravan even seven steps in its journey will be regarded in the sight of Allah as acceptable as those who perform the whole pilgrimage.

Many of the pilgrims die during this journey, partly from the effect of unfavorable climate of Arabia and partly from Asiatic cholera, the germs of which are proved to be always found in the water of Zemzem, the sacred well of Ishmael, which is asserted to have the supernatural power of cleansing all diseases and sins of the believers. Those who die during this journey are sure to be enrolled among the blessed martyrs and to enjoy the immediate reward of the heavenly presence.

It is believed that every year 80,000 pilgrims visit the Holy Temple; if the number be less than that

the angels descend from heaven and complete it.
Mohamet permitted the pilgrims to be engaged in
commerce on their way to and from Mecca.   This
attracts many people from Persia and India and other
parts of the Mohametan world to profit themselves
from these yearly religious fairs and bazars.   The
chances of highway robbery attract many believers
to rub their faces on the threshhold of the house of
Allah and make seven circuits a day around the
Kabeh, each time kissing the angel stone fallen from
heaven.

4. Alms and Tithes.   Alms is an important duty
demanded from a Moslem.   "Oh! merchants," says
Mohamet, "falsehood and deception are apt to pre-
vail in traffic; purify it, therefore, with alms; give
something in charity as an atonement, for God is
incensed by deceit in dealing, but charity appeases
his anger."   By observing the lives of Mohametans
one can easily see that they plunder and steal with
one hand and give alms with the other.   Such teachings as the above-quoted passage encourages them to
robbery.   A copper to a wayside beggar or a morsel
of bread to a dog is regarded the very means of puri-
fication of the soul.   The most bloody tyrant may
erect a mosque or a bridge with one part of the
money he has plundered from the Christians, and he
is noted as one of the benefactors of the human
race.   On his funeral day his coffin is carried over
the shoulders of thousands, and every believer passing by his grave stops a moment with high reverence
and deep admiration and repeats his prayer for the

illumination of that grave, the owner of which is already enrolled among the saints and authorized to mediate for the mortal creatures here below.

Two angels are said to accompany every Moslem, one on his right hand to record his good works and the other on his left hand to record his evil deeds. God is so tolerant for his chosen people that he permits one good action to be written ten times, while each bad action is not recorded for seven hours, which is an opportunity for repentance. By this holy decree a Moslem may steal ten dollars and give one dollar as alms and have his account all right in the book of the heavenly clerks, even without repentance.

5.   The Words of Testimony or the Creed of Islam. This is very brief and decisive. "La ilahe illallah, Muhammed er Resulullah." There is no deity but Allah. Mohamet is the apostle of Allah. So much power is attributed to this creed that one single utterance of it in a whole lifetime will be sufficient to secure Paradise. If a Moslem can not perform five daily prayers he is allowed to perform the Friday noon prayers. If he can not do it fifty times a year he may perform the two yearly prayers of the great festivals. In case he omits the same during his life he can utter the above-mentioned creed; if he can not do even that he may raise the forefinger of his right hand as a sign of this creed, and he is sure to be saved.

Mohametans assert that many Giaours, however obstinate in their lifetime, are compelled to submit at last to the true religion and make this significant

sign of the finger on their death-bed without letting
their friends know anything about it, and many are
so afraid of the flames of hell that they are obliged to
cry aloud, "There is no deity but Allah, Mohamet is
the apostle of Allah!"⁻ Some angels, whose special
service is to carry corpses from the graves of Giaours
to the graves of Moslems, come by night and take
the bodies of these converted believers to their respective places. We know nothing about such kind
of conversions, but positively testify to the fact that
over 100,000 Christians were willing to be butchered
during these last two years because of their unwill-
ingness to utter that single expression.

CHAPTER V.

THE MOHAMETAN THEOLOGICAL SCHOOLS.

1. **Ulemah, the Theological Party.** This is the most influential, the most fanatic, and the most dangerous element of the Mohametan world. Nurtured with the destructive spirit of the Koran, they are always ready and eager to indulge in a holy war and renew the formidable expeditions of Islam. Having the Sheikh al Islam (the religious head of Islam) as their leader, and the host of Softas, or Mollahs (the theological students), as their expert agents, and the civil and military parties as their helpers, and the whole Mohametan world as their followers, they plan and practice according to the interests of Islam. If the said head of Islam, being backed by his party, gives his legal decree for the dethronement of a sultan, the community cannot disregard it. That is why during these frequent changes of ministry and secret butcheries in the palace of the Sultan, the Sheikh al Islam is comparatively safe, and the coward Sultan favors the Softas and Mollahs, the chief actors in the late massacre at Constantinople, with presents, decorations and congratulations. On the day of Queen Victoria's jubilee celebration several cannons were discharged over the Bosphorus; when the Softas heard the first discharge they at once poured out into the streets holding their

47

bloody axes, clubs and daggers in their hands, eagerly inquiring whom they were to massacre, the Greeks or the Armenians.

2. **The Character of the Ulemah.** The general character of this religious party is corrupt and detrimental. They have only the Koran for their life-long study, and shutting themselves against any modern or external influence, and relying upon the fatalistic principles of Islamic philosophy, and indulging in cruel pleasures, they live a very depraved life.

They believe that every event of life, good or bad, is pre-ordained of God, and that no human agency can modify it. "On man's forehead," they say, "his personal destiny is written in a mysterious way that the guardian angels only can read it, and when his time is come they immediately take his soul; but before that appointed moment no enemy, no disease and no danger can cause death." This philosophy contradicts the idea of human freedom and responsibility, mortifies the aspiration towards the better, and leaves the energy of life as an instrument for the prevailing vice, corruption and oppression.

A language full of unimaginably corrupt expressions, a home discipline full of shameful inducements of hellish practices, a street life more wicked than that of Sodomite character, a religious teaching nothing more than a diabolic mechanism of cruelty, a pulpit advocating hatred and malice, a religious system of bloodshed and robbery, a book demoralizing the human likeness. This is the nearest description of the modern "Hell upon the earth." The

Hindoo and Chinese heathenisms have their standards of morality comparatively rational and pure; also have had their effects for the betterment of human civilization; but Islam's morality has been immorality, and the effect the destruction of humanity.

3. **Some Teachings of the Ulemah.** Besides the erroneous and harmful teachings of Islam mentioned in this book at various points, we will bring forth some ridiculous doctrines taught in the theological schools of Moslems; for example, as to the natural sciences:

The Origin of Apes. "When the mountain of Sinai was lifted up over the Israelites, and the law was given unto them, some among the people were disobedient and were entirely destroyed. But some part of the Jewish nation, rousing a rebellion against God on a sabbath day, were punished for their transgression by being changed into apes and driven away from the society of men, as an example for the contemporary and future generations." (*A different theory of evolution*).

Geography. "The earth, a flat body, rests between the horns of a huge ox, and the ox upon a cake of soap. When this animal slightly moves his head there is an earthquake." (Nobody can tell what will become of the earth when his feet slip off of the soap, which is not a safe foundation). The thunder is supposed to be the roar of the millstone that grinds oats for this huge animal of heavy burden.

The apparent heaven, a solid plate, is fastened up with four screws; at the time of the deluge God slightly touched one of them; at the end of this world all four will be taken out.

Physiology. For each kind of food there is a separate department in the stomach. Similar articles of food are changed into similar tissues in the human body. When God created each disease, he has appointed a vegetable near by it as a remedy or antidote. Lockman, the originator of medicine, was gifted by the power of hearing the voices of various plants as to what malady they were the remedy. Some favored persons have authority over the evil eyes and sicknesses, and can bind them with threads.

Chemistry. The four elements of nature are water, earth, air and fire. Gold is composed of three common articles, as copper, brass and mercury; if you know the proportion, and if you can find the mysterious powder which, mixed with the said minerals, produces gold, you can manufacture the precious metal. By burning certain mysterious incenses you can control the jealous spirits that watch day and night over the hidden subterranean treasures and possess boundless riches. Be careful to repeat certain prayers in order to avoid the strokes of those evil spirits.

4. **Supernatural Sciences Taught by Ulemahs.** —*About the Spirits.* In the air and among the stars numerous evil spirits, or demons, reside. Some of them are so enormous and powerful as to threaten the earth and the moon and the sun. Comets are the tails of these gigantic demons, and the eclipses of the moon and the sun are their struggle to swallow them, which can be avoided by crying to God from

the minarets, and at the same time frightening them by shooting fire-arms towards the skies and making all kinds of noises, by which the Turk succeeds every time in saving the poor moon from being swallowed.

Some of these evil spirits walk upon the earth, mostly among the graves and solitary caves. Some nights they take the appearance of a wrapped dead body and walk around to terrify innocent people. The public baths and the Christian churches are their especial gathering places by night, where, by horrible snorings, ugly laughters, hateful gestures, and dreadful dances they amuse themselves until the dawn of the day. Some of them are so ugly that when they laugh the lower lips rest upon the earth and the upper lips reach the stars.

The Size of the Angels. Angels exist in different sizes. Some are so small that 10,000 of them dwell upon a single hair of the Moslem's beard, and some are so large that their wings, when opened, reach from east to west, and some are still larger as to swallow all the water on the earth with a single gulp. Certain angels have certain services under the administration of Allah. Some are messengers, some guides, others clerks (to write the good and evil deeds of mankind and copy them in the heavenly register); others porters to carry dead bodies from one cemetery to the other; some are "soul takers," some are guardians of hell, etc. The space between the earth and God's dwelling place is a journey of fifty thousand years, which the angels perform in one day over the celestial stairs.

The Souls of Good Men, whether living or dead, have special privileges, as to have communion with Allah, to converse with Mohamet, to be present at distant places at the moment they desire, and to help the weakness of mankind. Many living or martyred Moslem saints are believed to ride on winged camels every Friday and go to Mecca to perform their noon-prayer at the Kabeh, and return the same day to their respective posts or graves. Mollah Hunkiar died 600 years ago, and, buried at Iconium (Asia Minor), is believed to make the same journey riding on a brick wall. Another martyred saint is regularly coming from Persia.

5. **Ulemah's Teachings About the Transactions Beyond the Grave.**—*The Interrogation in the Sepulchre.* This will be administered immediately after the burial of every Moslem by two angels upon the following four questions; 1. Who was thy Lord? 2. Who was thy Prophet? 3. Which was thy Religion? and 4. Which was thy Cubla (direction faced while in prayer)? He who will answer, Allah was my Lord, Mohamet my prophet, Islam my religion and Kabeh my Cubla, shall find a great illumination in his grave; but he who shall not make this proper answer shall be involved in darkness until the judgment day.

Resurrection. At the end of the world, when the archangel Israfil shall blow the trumpet, all things, even angels, men and devils, shall be annihilated. Then God will revive in, heaven first the "Angel of Death," who will recall all the souls in general and reunite them to their respective bodies. Upon the earth the first whom God will raise shall be Mahomet, upon whose shouting, "There is no deity but Allah, Mohamet is the apostle of Allah," all the believers shall come to life. One of the signs of the last day is that the sun shall rise from the west and go to the east.

The Judgment Day. God will then prepare a vast plain where all creatures will be summoned to give an account of their past conduct. The duration of that day shall be as long as a century, during which time the Giaours shall sigh and suffer great tribulation and anguish. As to the Moslems it will not be so, because those whose good works outweigh their recorded bad actions, shall immediately enter into Paradise; and those who are found lacking in the balance shall be favored by allowing their five large grave stones to be put on the scale of good actions and weighed again; if he still lacks, which will be very seldom, the good actions of the friends done in his behalf shall be brought forth and added upon the scale; also the prayers offered by his tomb shall be introduced to the account, and, in spite of all these favors, if his sins outweigh, he shall be sent to a temporary purgatory to be punished for the balance account; after which, through the intercession of his prophet, he shall be admitted into Paradise and enjoy the full pleasures thereof. Those whose scales shall be equally poised are to be detained in the middle space between Paradise and hell and pass their years of penance in that solitary place in a neutral condition.

Paradise. Mohametan paradise is nothing but an imaginary place of carnal gratifications. Nothing to do but to eat whatever you desire, which at once shall be created and brought before you; to drink wine and liquors which shall not disturb the mind; to enjoy the pleasure of numerous pearly damsels; to wear green silken robes which shall not wear out; to sit upon soft couches and talk with the friends you desire; to be served by blooming youths, and be happy by looking down and seeing the wretched condition of the Giaours in hell.

The Hell, as imaginary as the Heaven, is devided into seven stories; the first as a purgatory for Moslems, the second for Jews, the third for Christians, the fourth for Sabians, the fifth for Magians, the sixth for idolators, the seventh, and the lowest of all, for the hypocrites, who outwardly professed a religion but in reality had none. The essential means of torment are heat, cold, bitter foods and filthy drinks. The tree of Zakkum, which issues from the bottom of hell and the fruit of which resembles the heads of devils, is the only supply of food in hell with which the damned shall be obliged to fill their bellies, and being burnt of its bitterness shall cry for drink, when a mixture of filth and boiling sulphur shall be given unto them, which they shall be obliged to drink and vomit and begin the torment anew. When their skin is burned by the fire God will give them a new skin in order to perpetuate their torture. When they make complaint of heat they shall be exposed to extreme cold and vice versa.

During these ceaseless successions of extremities nineteen angels will take charge of the guardianship of hell not to let anybody escape from it, and to keep the fire and cold always in operation.

CHAPTER VI

1. **Dervishes and Their Doctrine.** Dervishes belong to a religious class or order professing self-denial and abstinence from worldly connections and luxuries, and spending their time in worship and religious meditation. Candidates of this order must prove themselves worthy by serving several months or years the Sheikh or the elder of the brotherhood, and by practicing at the same time the strict ordinances of the society. Dervish or Fakir means poor, and they glory in calling themselves "poor for the sake of the Truth (God)." But all dervishes are not poor. Some of them are really poor and destitute; they are called beggar dervishes, who go from town to town having nothing of their own but a patched robe and a lamb's or tiger's skin for their outer garment, sometimes barefooted and almost always bareheaded and wear long hair; in their hands a short stick with a battle-ax-shaped badge on one end; also a "Keshgoor," an oval dish, a large tambourine, a horn and long rosaries and some trifling relics or charms. For their daily bread they entirely depend upon the charity of the people. Some of them go silently in the market places and give thanks for anything that may be put in their oval dish. If they don't have enough they never com-

plain or ask for more. The majority of the beggar dervishes ask for charity by standing in the market places and repeating God's name, "Ya Hakk, ya Allah," O Truth! O God! constantly, and holding their Keshgoor, or horn, to persons they meet. Some of them sing while walking to attract the attention of the people; their good voice and significant poems are largely emotional and touching, as the soul's aspiration to reach the truth, vanities of this world and follies of a luxurious life or Jacob's lamentation over his lost son, Job's patience and deliverance, and sometimes praises of the martyred heroes, God's unchangeable will and the final destiny of the human soul.

2. **Resident Dervishes.** The majority of this order, however, are residents of the cities, having their own regular trades and families and properties. In their appearance they may be distinguished by green turbans around very high gray or white caps, long mantles and generally very long hair. They have various organizations, which they call certain "path" or "system." On certain nights during the week they come together at some mosque, or the Sheikh's department called "Tekkieh," convent or monastery, and spend hours in religious conversation. Especially on Thursday nights they hold a very long and fantastic meeting. First they sit on the floor in a circular form and begin to repeat the name of God (Hakk or Allah) with a low voice and in regular intervals of 50-70 in one minute. Gradually their enthusiasm in-

creases and their voices raise to a higher pitch. Then they come upon their knees, then stand upon their feet, and later they turn around in a circle, never omitting the regular repetition of God's name. After awhile they begin to whirl around the axis of their bodies, at the same time keeping the circular motion around the center, where they have their leader turning with the group and keeping the time of their gestures and howling. By this time some of them have fainted and fallen down, while the others continue with greater eagerness. Gradually others fall, still they continue until every one is exhausted. This practice, commonly united with the use of stimulants and narcotics, has a remarkably injurious effect upon the bodily health and mental soundness of the dervishes.

3. Dervishes as the Guardians of Shrines. Tekkiehs in the towns, smaller convents on the hill sides, the tombs of certain saints or martyrs, and the sacred spots of the past ages attract multitudes of visitors or pilgrims from every part of the Mohametan world. The visitors are sure to bring some presents or kill a sheep, in keeping with their requests and vows. Such places are regarded as centers of supplication for incurable maladies, mental and physical deformities, sterility, poverty, failure in business, and to gain love and favor. The water, the soil, the leaves, the fruits, the shadows of the trees, the wind and the sun of those places, are believed to have miraculous power. Such places are guarded by dervishes.

Some haughty sheikhs shut themselves in one of these sacred places and never go out of their walls for fifteen, twenty, thirty years. These "Fathers" are the living saints of the present age, and all the wealthy citizens and the eminent visitors are expected to go and kiss the skirts of his mantle and put their presents under his cushion. Even the greatest men would not sit in his presence but by his permission, and that on bended knees; and never talk freely, only answer his questions, and that very slowly and reverently; never smoke or drink coffee but by his special favor. These and their followers have a very great influence upon the transactions of the Government and private affairs of the sultans and their ministers. As a rule they are not so self-denying and abstinent as they profess to be.

4. **Mufties** are the men who alone have authority to apply Mohametan law to the practical transactions of daily life. They have the privilege to consult with the former books and extract their legal decrees from them. The following examples will illustrate their mode of administering the law:

A camel driver was once so angry with his camel that he swore to sell her for one mite by the first opportunity in the nearest city. After his anger was over he felt sorry for the oath he had made, but could not see any lawful way to escape from it. While in deep meditation he was advised by a friend to apply to the mufti of the town to see whether he could show a right way to settle this trouble. He went and stated the case. The mufti said, "Find a

cat and tie it to the tail of the camel and take them
into the market place and wait for the buyers. When
they ask the price say, 'The camel is for·one mite,
and the cat is for a thousand piastres, but I don't sell
them separately.' If they buy them for this price
you will lose nothing; if they don't buy you will be
free from your oath.''

Another man came to a mufti and said hesitatingly,
"My lord, while feeding in the pasture your ox hit
and killed mine, and I came to ask your excellency
whether you are obliged to repair my loss or not.''
The mufti, shaking his head as if feeling very sorry,
opened the hand-book of the law and read with a loud
voice the proposition that "the action of the animal
is null,'' and turning to the man said, "My son, they
were both mute animals and could not realize what
they did. I am sorry for the loss, but the law, as
you have heard, does not oblige me to undertake the
responsibility. Do not be grieved; whatsoever hap-
pens it is from God. Your ox was destined from
eternity to die in this way. Neither you nor I could
change it.'' The man returned hastily and said,
"Oh! I beg your pardon, my lord, it was my ox that
killed yours, and I was confused in my haste and
made the mistake.'' The pious mufti, with a
changed face and tone, said, "Wait a little; the
question has got confused. I must consult with the
larger book.''

When Sultan Aziz, the dethroned and murdered uncle
of the present Sultan, intended to visit Europe, a
puzzling difficulty arose in regard to the demands of the

Mohametan law that the soil upon which a Moslem sovereign may tread becomes a possession of Islam, and as the Giaour princes of Frankistan (Europe) could hardly be expected to submit to such a demand, there should be found some way to fulfil the law and enable the Sultan to carry out his intention. The leading religious authorities therefore held a solemn meeting in the palace to discuss the unprecedented subject. After much consideration one of them is said to have suggested the plan of preparing shoes for the Sultan having a layer of Turkish soil under them so that he could walk always upon his own country and not upon other lands. This plan came very near being agreed upon, when a brighter mufti said, "It would be more glorious for our religion to let the Sultan possess those countries and on his departure to make presents of them to their former owners." This was unanimously approved and offered to the Sultan.

CHAPTER VII.

1. **Biblical References of Armenia.** Armenia is a high table land on the southern slope of the Caucausus, between the Caspian· and Black seas and Mesopotamia. Its boundaries have varied at different times of its history. It is believed by the greatest majority of the Biblical scholars to be the first seat of the human race, and also the cradle of mankind after the deluge. The four rivers mentioned in the second chapter of Genesis: Pison (the present Joruk that runs to the Black Sea), Gihon (the present Arax that runs to the Caspian Sea), Tigris and Euphrates (both run to the Persian Gulf), have their sources in the highlands of Ararat, Armenia. According to the modern critics, Armenia was formerly called Ararat, after the name of that illustrious mountain, about 17,000 feet high, upon which the ark of Noah rested after the abatement of the waters. The fertile soil, the magnificent scenery, the mild and healthy climate, the large rivers, and the "one thousand sources" of pure waters, make it worthy to be called the "Garden of Eden."

Other Biblical references in connection with Armenia: In II. Kings, 19:37, and Isa., 37:38, we notice that the sons of Sennacharib, the Assyrian monarch, after killing their father (681 B. C.), "escaped into the land of Armenia." Again

62

in Ezek., 27:14 and 38:6, Armenia is indicated under the name of Togarmah, the great grandson of Noah, to whom the Armenians carry their descendance, as furnishing Tyre with horses and mules, a product for which it is still noted. Tigranes I., the celebrated Armenian king, is said to have been an ally of Cyrus the Great in overthrowing the Babylonians and thus in liberating the Jews from their seventy years' captivity. A foreshadow of this event is indicated by the prophet Jeremiah (51:27-29; also 50:41, 42): "Call together against her the kingdoms of Ararat, Minnie and Ashkanaz," etc.

2. About the Origin of the Armenian Nation there are two different opinions. The one, so long cherished by the Armenians themselves, is that their ancestor, Haig, the son of Togarmah and the fifth generation from Noah, a hero, and a worshiper of the true Jehovah, lived in Babylonia, where one of the giants, coming into power, called himself Bel or Baal and claimed for himself the divine worship. Haig did not recognize him, and after slaying him in a struggle left the country and fled with his men to the mountainous regions on the north, and established there a principality which was named Hai or Haigazian, the title which Armenians still use for themselves. The name Armenian is supposed to be given by foreigners, after the name of the seventh great Armenian ruler, Aram.

The other opinion lately brought forward is that the Armenian nation, belonging to the Aryan race, came from the north, from Caucasia, and did not

occupy the country before the seventh century B. C.
They followed the track of the Medes, owing to the
gradual decline of the Assyrian Empire.   The arguments in favor of this theory are the facts that the
Armenians in their physiognomy and natural con-
struction and in their traditions and language have
close connection and resemblance with other Aryan
nations, which would be the contrary if they had an
Assyrian or Chaldean origin.   The Armenian language has not the slightest resemblance of the Se-
mitic branch, Assyrian, Chaldean, Phœnician,
Hebrew and Arabic; while many original words and
other characteristics of the language show the evident identity with the Indo-Germanic (European)
branch — for instance, Mayer, mother; Douster,
daughter; Hair, hair; Vod, foot; Gow, cow; Luce,
light; Dour, door; Gadou, cat; Bardes, paradise;
Dev, day; Ash, ass; Anoun, noun, and many others.

3. **Armenia According to the Ancient Foreign
Historians.**   In the famous inscriptions of the
Achæmanides (the ancient Persian monarchs, as
Darius, Hystaspes, Xerxes, Artaxerxes, and others)
in Persepolis (the ancient Persian capital of the said
dynasty and afterward ruined by Alexander the
Great) the name of Armenia is found written in
various forms, and the pictures of Armenian tribu-
taries are represented as marching after the Cappa-
docians to render homage to the great Persian king;
the probable date, six centuries before Christ.

Herodotus, the oldest Greek historian, born 484
B. C., also mentions the absorption of the Armenian

kingdom in that of Darius, and the exaction of a tribute of four hundred talents.

Xenophon, the celebrated Greek general, historian and philosopher, born 445 B. C., in his account of the adventurous retreat of the Greeks in the East, known in history as "The Retreat of the Ten Thousand," throws much light upon the ancient Armenians and Kurds.

Armenia was included in the conquests of Alexander the Great, 320 B. C., and after his death at the partition of his kingdom Armenia was submitted to the Seleucidæ of Syria. But in 190 B. C. she revolted against the Syrian King, Antiochus the Great, and gained her independence through the aid of the Parthian king, Mithridates I., who appointed his brother, Valarsaces, over Armenia. This was the beginning of the second period of the Armenian Kingdom.

4. **The Four Periods of the Armenian Kingdom.** The first period, beginning with Haig and ending at the time of Seleucidæ, embraces about 22 centuries. The first part of this period is legendary, or rather, unknown. The second period begins with Valarsaces, 190 B. C., and goes until 390 A. D., embracing a period of nearly 600 years. The greatest event of this period is the evangelization of the whole nation, about which the reader will find a concise information in the next chapter. The greatest king of this period was Tigranes II., who was able to fight with the Roman rulers. After him Tacitus, the historian, says the Armenians were almost always

at war with the Romans through hatred, and with the Parthians through jealousy, until the two great enemies prevailing over Armenia divided it between themselves, 390 A. D.

Between the second and the third periods, about 500 years, the Armenians were subjected partly to the Roman or Greek Empire and partly to the Persian kingdom and Mohametan caliphate.

The third period begins at 859 A. D. and comes to its end at 1045 A. D., thus embracing about 200 years.

The fourth period of the Armenian independence (1045-1393) was confined to Cilicia. Ruben, a relative of the last king of the third period, escaped into Cilicia and established the Rubenian kingdom, having the city of Sis for his capital. The mountainous situation of Cilicia helped the Armenians to keep their independence until 1393, when Leon VI., the last king of this dynasty, an exile by the Mohametan caliphate, died at Paris, France, and was buried in the Cathedral at St. Denis. Zeitoun of the present day is the last spark of this local independence.

According to the above statements the Armenian Kingdom began at twenty-fourth century B. C. and ended at fourteenth century A. D., thus embracing a period of nearly 3,800 years with about 600 years' intervals of subjection, during which time they were governed by provincial system, which can not be called total subjection with the present meaning of the word. During the last centuries Armenia became gradually divided between Turkey, Russia and

Persia. The Ottoman Turks nominally conquered Armenia, but until recent times (1847) it was practically under various Kurdish Sheiks, or chiefs.

The present number of the Armenians is supposed to be over four millions: 2,500,00 in Turkey, 1,500,-000 in Russia and 150,000 in Persia. It was over twelve millions when subjugated by the Mohametans, but reduced to one-third by unceasing persecutions and frequent massacres, about which read the subsequent chapters.

CHAPTER VIII.

THE ARMENIAN CHURCH.

1. Pre-Christian Religion of Armenia. From the ancient Armenian literature, consisting of national songs, only a few quotations are left, and the earliest inscriptions on the great citadel rock of Van have not yet been satisfactorily made out. What we understand from the authorities existing is that the Armenians, before Christianity, worshiped the heavenly bodies, the sun, the moon and the stars, and the fire, like other surrounding nations. The names of many places and persons, still in use, are the various derivations of the names of these deities. The relics of those ages of heathenism, however, show that their idolatry was not of the coarser and abominable sort. So far as we know, polygamy, human sacrifice and immoral practices in worship were not introduced nor practiced among the Armenians; on the other hand, the sacredness of family life, the fidelity in marriage, the obedience to parents, national enthusiasm, attachment to the "fatherland," social habits, industry, peacefulness, hospitality, and most of all religious zeal and piety—still prevailing characteristics of the race—are traced back to those remote ages. Haig, the supposed ancestor of the nation, is described as "the eagle of the mountains of Ararat," the first hero who ever declared himself for freedom and conscience. His grandson, Aramais, who has built stores of luxuries for himself, is condemned for gluttony, and his hateful character was put into a proverb and passed through generations. The seventh ruler from Haig, Ara the Beautiful (the son of Aram, after whom the nation was named "Armenian"), was highly praised, not only for his personal beauty but chiefly for his fidelity to his nation and temperate firmness against the worldly and impure intentions of the Assyrian Queen Semiramis (Shamiram), even at the expense of his life, which he lost while bravely fighting with the hordes of this ancient Jezebel. Armenian virgins are described as gathering in the Temple of the Goddess of Purity and singing the virtues of virginity and matrimonial fidelity. Heripsimian virgins fled to Armenia as the safest shelter to preserve their honor against the vicious tyranny of the Roman rulers. Santookhd, the only daughter of the Armenian King in the first century A. D., was converted to christianity by the Apostle Thaddeus, declined all the glories of a wordly crown, and in spite of the appeals, promises and threatenings of her idolatrous father, kept the true faith until her innocent blood, together with that of her apostle, was shed on the beautiful plains of Shavarshan, where roses and lilies are believed to bloom out of her blood. These were the ideals of the Armenian nation, even before Christianity was fully accepted among them.

2. **Evangelization of the Armenian Nation.** Christianity was undoubtedly introduced among the Armenians early in the second century of our era,

and towards the end of the third century it was officially proclaimed as the national religion of the country. According to the traditions of the Armenian church, the Armenian King Abcarius, having a chronic malady, and hearing about the miracles of Jesus, sent special messengers to him with a letter, and invited the Saviour to come and live in his capital Edessa (the present Ourfa) and be safe from the enmity of Jewish authorities. Our Lord, the tradition continues, highly appreciated this kind feeling of hospitality, but as he could not go himself he promised to send one of his apostles after his resurrection, which he did by sending Thaddeus, called the Apostle of Armenia. Nobody can tell how much truth or probability there is in this tradition, but that Thaddeus and Bartholomew were sent to the northeastern regions and established there Christian churches, and that among the Armenians many converted Christians were persecuted and some churches were destroyed through the influences of the great anti-Christian emperors of the Roman commonwealth, are historical facts. Still the general evangelization of Armenia dates towards the end of the third century.

The historical founder of the Armenian church was Saint Gregore "the Illuminator," an Armenian prince, related to King Tiridates, who during the first part of his reign was a great persecutor of "the new faith transplanted from Judea." The young prince Gregore, resigning his wordly position, consecrated himself to the enlightenment of his people in spite of all the difficulties and severe persecutions he suffered from the people and the king. Tiridates being very anxious to change his mind and course, shut him in a dungeon for several years, but could not prevent the rapid progress of the flame of Christianity which was already consuming the remains of the pagan ages. The most cruel thing attributed to Tiridates was his killing some maiden refugees, who, persecuted by the Roman emperor, had fled to Armenia for shelter. His remorse and shame of this guilt was so strong that he is related to have lost his mind for some time, until one night in his dream he saw the graves of the said martyrs illuminated by a bright light, and upon this vision he at once released Saint Gregore and was baptized by him with all his subordinates, and proclaimed Christianity to be the religion of his dominions. Soon churches were established and the visionary light which was believed to illumine the graves of the martyrs was spread over the country; and at the very site of that heavenly light a magnificent church was erected by the name of "Echmiadzin," the Descent of the Only Begotten, which is until this day the most sacred headquarter of the Armenian church and the seat of the highest religious authority called "Catholicos of the Whole Armenians." (276 A. D.)

Saint Gregore, the Illuminator, being consecrated Bishop of Armenia in 302 A. D., was the first Catholicos or father of that sacred seat, and uninterrupted succession is kept until this day. The present head of the Armenian church is His Holiness Mugerditch

Khrimian, the honored and the beloved Archbishop. The Bible was translated into the Armenian language early in the fifth century by Mesrob, who also invented and introduced the present alphabet, composed of thirty-six letters. (Three more letters were introduced afterwards for foreign sounds.)

3. **The Relation of the Armenian and Greek Churches.** Though Christianity was introduced first among the Jews and the Greeks, the Armenian church has the honor of being "the First National Church in Christendom." Nothwithstanding her national independence, she acknowledged the church universal and conducted herself in unity with the sister churches in the East, the principal one of which was the Greek church. St. Gregore, the Illuminator, was trained and even ordained in the Greek school at Cæsaria, and was authorized to represent the Armenian branch of "the Church Universal" in the general councils. The early history of the Christian church shows that the Armenian delegates of these councils had their own share in the discussions of various theological and ecclesiastical subjects; so much that the Western delegates and the Bishop of Constantinople, and even the Emperor Constantine himself, could not help to admire and appreciate their superior intellect and zeal for the interest of the church. Especially at the celebrated discussions of Arius' doctrine against the divine nature of our Saviour, the Armenian bishops, as opponents to that heresy, expressed the greatest zeal for the preservation of the old orthodox doctrine. And the Necean

creed that was arranged as a protest and defense against the erroneous teaching of Arius was at once adopted by the Armenian church and used in her worships until this day. Saint Gregore, the Illuminator, added to it some sentences in order to emphasize its general spirit.

The Council of Chalcedon, 451 A. D., the Armenian bishops could not attend on account of the Persian persecutions, and not being contented with the resolution of that Council in regard to the number of the natures of our Saviour, refused its decrees in 536. Accepting the Mono-physical Doctrine (that is, in our Lord's person the divine and the human united to one unseparable nature), she proclaimed herself independent of the Greek church, and since then had no formal union with her, although she regards her as a "sister church." This separation, in spite of its political disadvantages, has proved beneficial for the maintainance of the purity of the doctrines and the practice of the Armenian church.

The seven sacraments of the early church, as mass, confession, absolution, unction, matrimony, baptism and eucharist, though practiced in the Armenian church, are rather formal than doctrinal, as is proved by her susceptibility to internal reformation. The following hymn, composed by Nerses the Graceful, the Armenian Archbishop who lived in the twelfth century (about 400 years before the Reformation of Martin Luther), and sung in the Armenian church until this day, is one among many that shows the doctrine and spirit of that ancient church:

O, dawning brightness! Sun of righteousness! Shine forth upon
  me.
Fatherly issue (spirit), in my heart renew pleasing words for
  thee.
Treasure of bounties, thine hidden riches grant my soul to see.
Open mercy-door to confessing soul, with heavenlies rank me.
Thou one in three, Carer all that be, on me have mercy.
Arise Lord helping, raise the slumbering, like angels to be,
Eternal Father, Co-existent Son, ever ghost holy,
Loving name Jesus, with thy love bruise my heart-stony.

CHAPTER IX.

After conversion to Christianity the history of the Armenian nation has become largely the history of the church; for, being situated beyond the frontiers of christendom, they suffered constant persecution from the surrounding heathen nations, and the State was obliged to defend the church at any cost.

1. Persecution From Persians. Towards the middle of the fifth century, as it was mentioned in the first chapter, Armenia had lost its national independence, and one part of it was ruled by Persians, though in a provincial system. The Persians who were bigoted Zoroastrian fire worshipers, aimed at this time the conquest and the conversion of the world. Accordingly, in 450 A. D. the Persian King dictated a letter to the Armenian princes setting forth the superiority of fire worship to Christianity, and inviting the whole nation to accept it. Upon this threatening invitation a great council was held, in which clergy and laymen sat together and a unanimous reply of refusal was decided upon. The exact copy of that remarkable answer was preserved by one of the bishops who signed it. After intelligibly refuting the false arguments of the Persian King against Christianity, they said in conclusion: "From this faith no one can move us, neither angels nor men, neither sword nor fire, nor water nor any deadly

75

punishment. If you allow us our faith we will
accept no other lord in place of you, but we will
accept no God in place of Jesus Christ; there is no
other God beside him.   If after this solemn confession you ask anything more of us, lo, we are before
you and our lives are in your power; from you torments, from us submission; your sword, our necks;
we are not better than those who are gone before us,
who gave up their possessions and their life for this
testimony."

The haughty King of Persia, being enraged by the
boldness of this reply, ordered an army of 200,000
men against this small country, which stood alone in
front of a vast power.   The battle, often called the
Armenian Marathon, was fought on the plain of
Avarair under Mt. Ararat.   In this desperate struggle the much smaller army of the Armenians was
defeated, and their leader Vartan, the Brave, was
killed, but the surprising resistance offered by rich
and poor, by men, women and children, convinced
the King of Persia that he might crush the Armenians, but could never make fire-worshipers of them;
and was obliged to admit the declaration of the High
Priest of fire worship, that " These people have put
on Christianity, not like a garment, but like their
own flesh and blood.   They are not afraid of fetters
and torments, nor care for property, and choose
death rather than life.   Who can stand against them?"

2.   **The Bravery of the Armenian Women During
This Persecution.**   The above mentioned historian
Bishop, who was an eye-witness of this terrible war-

fare that reduced the country almost to a desert, describes the condition of the Armenian women at that time, saying: "I cannot enumerate all the wives of the heroes, both of those who were in fetters and those who had fallen in battle. All of them being kindled by a holy ambition, put on the same virtue of fidelity. The delicately reared women went untiringly to the houses of prayer on foot and bare-footed, asking by vows that they might be enabled to endure their great affliction. The everlasting Psalms were the words of their lips, and their complete comfort was in the reading of the prophets. With their eyes they saw the spoiling of their goods, and with their ears they heard the moans of suffering of their dear ones. With prayers they opened the closed doors of heaven, and with holy petitions caused the angels of redemption to descend. With their hands they worked and were fed, and the pensions granted them by the court they sent year by year to their husbands and sons for their comfort. The snows of many winters melted, the springs came, the life-loving men saw and rejoiced; but they never could see those for whom they longed. To outsiders they appeared mourning and sorrowful widows, but in their own souls they were adorned with heavenly love. Their desires and prayers to God were only that they might finish their course with faith and courage, filled with heavenly love, even as they had begun."

3. **Persecutions From the Mohametans.** After the fall of the Persian kingdom in the seventh cen-

tury Armenia was invaded by the Saracens, the Mohametan warriors, for about 200 years. The history of this time was not brighter than any period of religious persecutions the Armenians had suffered. In the choice of Islam, or sword, or low subjection, Armenians have always chosen one of the last two proposals. While the fury of Islam was overwhelming Persia, Turkey and India were progressing with wholesale conversions of races and tribes. The Armenians proved themselves to be the only exception, and to break off these rapid and sure conquests. If they could not be permitted to live for their friends and country they would prefer death to Islam, hence the saying prevailed among Mohametans as a proverb that, "The old obstinate Armenian will not become Musliman."

After the withdrawal of the Saracens, owing to the fall of the caliphate in Bagdad, the Armenians gained their independence under the third period of their kingdom. But the land could not gain her rest from the repeated invasions of proselyted Moslem tribes, especially the Tartars. By the short-sighted policy of the Greek emperors, the Armenian kingdom was overthrown in 1045 A. D., and thus the whole eastern frontier was laid open to the invasion of the Seljouk Tartars, who might have been successfully resisted by the hardy mountaineers of Armenia. The result was fatal, both to Armenia, which was overrun, and to the Greek empire; for in the battle of 1071 A. D. the Emperor Romanus IV. was defeated and made prisoner by Alp Arslan, and the

whole of Asia Minor was left to the mercy of the merci-
less Seljoukian Tartars, who, as most bigoted
Mohametans, scourged the country for 200 years.

Genghis Khan, the Mongolian invader, early in the
thirteenth century, dealt' comparatively better with
the Armenians, which the Mohametans attributed to
the influence of his wife, who was a Christian.   But
after the overthrow of his temporary dominion the
Armenians suffered more from the vengeance of the
Egyptian caliphate.   The exact cause of this vengeance was the hospitality the Armenians showed to
the Crusaders, sheltering and feeding them a whole
winter on their way to the Holy Land to recover it
from the hands of Mohametans.   The cruelties of
Timourlane, the Tartar, devastated Armenia at the
close of the fourteenth century; his bloody soldiers
being tired of killing, buried many Armenians alive,
or drove them into the rivers, and many children and
women together were drowned.   In 1605 Shah Abbas,
of Persia, forcibly transplanted 12,000 Armenian
families to his country as slaves to serve the good
pleasure of the Mohametan Persians.   From that
time on the Armenians have suffered continuous and
severer persecutions from the Kurds and the Turks,
the description of which is given in subsequent
chapters.

Armenia, owing to its geographical situation, has
always been the battlefield of the eastern and western
invasions.   Her importance in the history of civilization and the Christian church was that, she being at
the frontier of Christendom, has done much in check-

ing the fury of the barbarous invaders, and more perhaps in suffering for the freedom and religion of their western brothers, who, had it not been for this providential stronghold, would not be able to have time and facility in developing their civilization, both secular and ecclesiastical.

CHAPTER X.

1. **Armenians Are an Exceedingly Religious People.** You cannot find a single member in that communion who has not been baptized in the sacred fount of the church and in the name of the Holy Trinity; not one in ten thousand whose marriage is not performed under the authority of the church. If there be any they are refused to approach the Lord's table and their children are not admitted to baptism, and their dead are not buried with christian ceremonies. In every Armenian town the best building is the church, with the sign of the cross on its top. The choicest lamb in the flock is offered at the threshold of the holy convent; the highest seat in the house and the best portion on the table is for the priest. The most secret affairs and sorrows are entrusted to the fatherly confidence of the pastor. On each visit all the members of the family are glad to hold his hand and reverently kiss it while he utters "God bless you." The aged men and women, in many instances deprived of sight, with remarkable regularity attend the services in the church, which are performed twice a day, very early in the morning and late in the afternoon, repeating silently all the way the beautiful psalms which they learned in their youth. When they meet a friend on their way from

81

the church the ready blessing of their mouth is
"God be merciful unto your soul."

On Sunday mornings the great assembly of men
and women in the church reverently stand up while
the priest is officiating the holy sacrament; and the
children, arrayed in white robes with red crosses on
them, and holding lights in their hands, turn around
the main altar sweetly singing: "Lift up your
heads, O, ye gates, and be ye lifted up, ye everlasting doors; and the king of glory shall come in." In
the presence of such a scene one is reminded of
the heavenly seraphin and cherubin which turn day
and night around the throne of the Almighty.

2. **The Passion Week in the Armenian Church.**
After celebrating the glorious entrance of our Saviour
into Jerusalem on Palm Sunday and following the
events of the first part of the week, on Thursday
afternoon twelve priests and deacons sit together
before the main altar, and imitating the significant
events of the upper room in Jerusalem, one of them,
the highest in rank, girds the apron, a sign of
humility, and approaches the company of twelve,
and one by one wash their feet, at the same time
repeating portions of the farewell speech of our
Lord. One of them taking Peter's part seems too
humble to let the Great Master wash his feet, but
being persuaded of its necessity, submits himself to
the will of the Master.

At midnight of the same evening, while the
scene of the crucifixion is represented with ideal
solemnity and sincere piety, all the candles are put

out, and Mary, the afflicted mother, clinging to the foot of the cross, begins to weep and wail through the melodious voice of the best singer in the choir. All the women in the galleries burst into tears of grief, and words of repentance are heard on every side until the blessed mother submits herself to the divine will, and the last word of the bleeding Saviour is heard upon the cross, " It is finished." The name of this ceremonious night is " Come and Weep."

When the service of the crucifixion is over, about two hours before sunrise, many people go right away to the cemetery and put candles over all the graves in order to illuminate the valley of death. The outward appearance, how impressive and silent! the spiritual meaning is more instructive and full of comfort. The sweet remembrance of the passed friends is more sweet with the meditation of "the new sepulchre in the garden." The rest of the day passes in reverent quiet.

The Easter services begin on Saturday evening, and at the end of the long and ceremonious services the officiating priest gives the good tidings of the day: " Christ has risen from the dead," and the attendants respond: "Blessed is the resurrection of Christ." Friends meeting with each other during the three days of Easter use the above two sentences for their salutation. The priest is sure to visit each home in his parish, holding a very brief service in each.

3. **Armenians Have Always Been Industrious and Progressive,** and kept the highest position among the

Eastern races in regard to their ability in commerce, trade, agriculture and letters. Their language, with its somewhat difficult pronunciation, excels all the dialects of the East, and in its syntax and word-making capacity equals Greek or Latin. Its adaptation to the Christian ideas is remarkable. It is a proverbial saying that " the Arabic is fit to swear, Kurdish to quarrel, Turkish to curse, while the Armenian is to pray.'' Soon after the conversion of the nation to Christianity, the Armenian young men flocked into the highest institutions at Athens, Constantinople, Edessa and other centers of education. While Mohamet was spending his solitary hours in shaping the immense mouths of the ugliest demons, or describing the devil-headed fruits of the infernal plantation, the Armenians were struggling for prosperity and development. Upon the fertile land and among the largest rivers they always clung to the plough, and led their flocks in the green pastures of Armenia. Grains and varieties of fruits were exchanged for the other necessities of life, and their commercial enterprises extended to the foreign countries. In spite of ceaseless persecutions and spoils, Armenia has always had her princes, wealthy and able merchants and very skillful traders. Each father regarded his essential duty to train his son in his own trade and perpetuate the source of wealth. Each mother taught her daughter economical housekeeping and industry. There has been no time in the history of Armenia when her children assaulted her neighbors, or gave themselves to luxury and idleness,

After so much trouble and suffering their existence and position must and does have some significance.

4. **One of the Characteristics of the Armenian People** is very strong attachment to the family life and "fatherland." The type of the family is patriarchal. The old father and mother, with their grown sons and their families, sometimes numbering altogether forty to sixty, live in the same house, the grandfather being the ruler and the grandmother the manager. Young and modest brides, being taught from their early childhood, are always obedient and diligent, too modest to speak aloud before the grand-father and elder brothers-in-law. When the old father eats, the brides are eager to wait on him. When he wants to go out they bring his out-door shoes and help him to put them on and take them off when he comes in, and get his good words of bless-ing for all these services. When the morning work is done and the men leave the house for their field or shop the young mother sits beside the cradle and sings softly as she sews, knits or spins:

Awake, and open thy beauteous eyes, my child, my little one!
Thy mother sees therein her life, her glory and her sun.
Thou shalt grow up, grow tall and strong, as rises in the air a
    stately palm tree; how I love thy stature tall and fair!
The heroes of Mount Ararat, their ghosts shall strengthen thee
    with power and might that thou as brave as Vartan's self
    mayst be.
Awake and ope thy beauteous eyes, my child, my little one!
Thy mother sees therein her life, her glory and her sun.

And no wonder if these first impressions pressed upon the mind of the baby and make him attached to his "good mother," the "dear home" and "sacred fatherland.'' He is the joy of his mother, the protector of his sister, the lover of his wife, the server of his church and the martyr of his fatherland, so full of charming scenery and sacred memories.

The ideal and the highest ambition of the Armenian is, and always has been, and always will be, Liberty in his home-land. The accumulation of wealth is not their highest desire, though they have rare chances and natural ability for that. The luxuries of life are not the greatest attraction for them, though they have the worst example before their eyes. The theory of fatalism has never been a favorite idea with the Armenians, though it broods all over Asia. The ambition has never stirred them to aggress the rights of their neighbors, though they have had many chances in their long national life to do so. They are, and always have been contented, temperate, practical and peaceful. They loved liberty, they were always ready to protest against a despotic spirit. This spirit of protest caused them to be superficially called ''Anmiapan,'' ''Discordant,'' but every freedom-lover knows that

> The path of freedom is thorny all the way,
> So many trials and strifes do happen every day;
> Too straight and narrow is this world for thee
> If thou art a lover of Liberty.

CHAPTER XI.

1. **The Intended Bride.** Among the Armenians marriage is at an age earlier than in western countries—19 for boys and 15 for girls may be regarded a medium age for marriage. The engagement takes place earlier than that, sometimes when the couple are too young to understand the meaning of "the cradle contract." The parents are the chief operators in this. When a boy reaches his fifteenth or seventeenth year, his parents, especially the mother, the sisters and the aunts, begin to talk among themselves about a proper candidate for *their* future bride. Dark and large eyes, long and brown hair, rosy cheeks and round face and medium stature are desired for her physical qualities; diligence, modesty, manual skill, respectable parentage and good name for the moral qualities. The education, however, is not regarded essential, especially in the interior. In their research for a proper candidate they very often carry their mission and consultation beyond the borders of the family circle—it may be whispered in the church, in the marriage feasts, at the public baths, and on the streets. They make unexpected calls to the home of the girl under their consideration, the object of which is to examine the condition of the house and the manners of the girl, etc. When they

87

approve one the subject is taken into more serious consideration among all the members of the family, and the opinion of the young man is consulted. He is too bashful to state his thoughts freely, especially in his father's presence, but he finds many ways to express himself. The young lady and her family are considered formally unaware of the intention, though they actually know about the case and prepare themselves to respond to the proposition. The girl has less voice than the young man, still her decision can not be entirely overlooked.

2. **The Ceremony of Engagement.** When the friends of the young man give their decision for a certain young woman, they send some friends or their priest to make the formal proposition and get the answer of "the other side." If they get a favorable reply a day is appointed for the ceremony of engagement, when the friends of the young man, associated with the priest, go to the home of the young woman to perform the ceremony of engagement. The nearest friends of both families are there, but neither of the couple. After some pell mell conversation, the representative of the young man asks the elder member of the girl's family, "Mr. ———, do you know for what purpose we came here this evening?" He answers, "You are all welcome; what purpose can we expect but friendship and brotherly call. You know our house is always open for the friends; you are a thousand times welcome." "Yes, indeed, we are friends, and always welcomed in your house. God bless you and your home, but in this visit we

have a special purpose, and, the Lord willing, a good purpose, and we are sure that you will not disappoint us." The girl's friends must never show themselves acquainted with the said purpose or anxious for its discussion; therefore, must always repeat the same general words of welcome and friendship, until the representative of the young man opens the question and says, "Mr. ——, by the will of God we came to beg your favor in giving your noble daughter, Mary, to your servant, our son James. We expect that you will not refuse our proposal and send us away disappointed." After some formal hesitation and repetitions of the proposal the question is referred to the oldest member of the young woman's family, who says, "You are welcome a thousand times, if it is the Lord's will, may it be blessed for us all." This answer being equal to "yes," is responded to with great joy and congratulations, and the young woman being called in, the presents of the young man—pieces of gold coins, heavy embroidered handkerchiefs, a gold ring, etc.—presented to her. Her silent acceptance of these things is regarded the sign of her consent for the contract, after which the priest rehearses some words of prayer and vows in behalf of the contractors, then a good supper is served. In larger towns the young man may accompany the friends for the ceremony of engagement. Between the times of engagement and wedding the couple do not see nor write to each other—only the parents give visits on special days, as Christmas and Easter, or other occasions, and send presents to each other. The presents of the groom are expected to be more valuable and frequent. The bride is expected to furnish the groom and his nearest friends with embroideries, stockings and other articles, all made by her own hand. Also she has to prepare several suits for herself, all to be used after marriage. The wedding garments, however, silken and of any color but white, are to be prepared by the groom.

3. **The Wedding.** The families of the bride and groom make special preparations for the wedding and invite their relatives and friends and neighbors to their respective homes two or three days before the marriage. One hundred guests in each home can be regarded a moderate estimate. A feast is served in both homes on the afternoon of the marriage day, after which the family and guests of the groom, all with lighted candles in their hands, go to the home of the bride "to take the bride," as they say. After spending about an hour with the guests there, and partaking of "sherbet," (non-alcholic drink) and fruits, they take the bride to the home of the groom, or to the church, where the religious ceremony is performed by the priest. The ceremony takes about an hour, and sometimes more. Nobody among the friends of the bride except one lady attends the marriage ceremony in the church, and the members of her family do not come to see her in her new home within ten to fifteen days, and she does not go to visit them before thirty to forty days.

In various parts of Armenia they have different customs, e. g.: In some places each guest brings with her or him a small sum of money or other provisions to meet the wedding expenses. In some places they do not use invitation cards, but send a messenger to each friend's house, or distribute pieces of candy with a message of "salutations." In many places on the marriage-feast day the gates are opened to the poor and strangers. The jewelry presented to the bride by the groom are pieces of gold coins of various value, as $1 to $15 apiece worn as a necklace. On the day after the marriage the friends bring gifts, such as rugs and copper vessels, and from a saucer to a wash-tub. A few days before and after the marriage the groom is called by the name of "King" and another young man will associate him as his "Prime Minister," and a little boy "the groom's brother." In many places the bride has to wear a veil for months or years after her departure from her father's home. The new bride, beginning from the engagement day, is not allowed to speak before her father-in-law, brothers-in-law and their nearest relatives for several months or years after the marriage. If they are obliged to tell something they either speak into the ears of a child of the family, who repeats it aloud, or they themselves express it by signs. In the interior, men and women do not eat together, especially when there is a stranger in the house.

The Armenian church never allows divorce for any cause; only permits separation without re-marriage. A god-child can never marry his or her godfather's children. The common priests of the Armenian çhurch must be married men before they are ordained, but neither the priest nor his wife can marry a second time.

The marriage feasts are generally accompanied with music and singing and fire-works, and similar amusements.   Once in a Protestant community, when they were taking the groom and the bride from the church back to the home, they sang on the way, "Jesus, I my cross have taken."

CHAPTER XII.

THE ARMENIANS' CONDITION IN THE FIRST HALF OF THIS CENTURY.

1. The Local Governments. The nature of the Turkish Government, especially in the provinces, was until very recently somewhat like a feudal system. The local beys (noblemen), or sheikhs or pashas, had their own arbitrary rule in certain districts, and very often would fight with each other, or even with the central government. The sultans of the last two centuries, being politically impotent and devoted to sensual gratifications, abandoned the task of administration to the favorites and parasites of the palace, who had access to the sale of public function as the readiest mode of performing it, and the most profitable for themselves. Armenia was not an exception to other provinces, but was more unfortunate in being abandoned to Kurdish authorities. The Kurds, supposed to be the descendants of the ancient Parthians, are a bloody and semi-savage race, nominally governed or rather led by various local sheikhs or chiefs, and always plundering the Armenians and Nestorian Christians, with whom they lived for centuries. Most of them belong to the Persian sect of Mohametan religion, and some tribes still keep the traces of ancient pantheism and fire-worship, and even the devil-worship. While the population of Armenia proper was in this condition, other Armenians in Lower Armenia and Cilicia were subjected both to the central government and local Turkish beys or agas, every one of whom was a king in his own circle and dealt with their rayas (subjects) as a rule very unjustly and, in many cases, very unwisely for themselves. None of these local governors had any project for the future welfare of the country. Every one acted as if the end of the world was at hand; their motto was, "Impoverish the people in order to enrich yourself." If they had any activity other than robbing and degrading their rayas it was in the line of quarreling with rival chiefs at any expense of life and property. At any moment the aga of the next town could be expected to come with his "segmen" (horsemen) and open a dispute with the chief of this town, shed blood, burn a part of the town, carry away the herds and flocks, spoil the crops and do every harm imaginable. Whether defeat or victory, the people always lost, and the greatest sufferers were the Armenians. The Kurdish or Turkish bey would send word to certain Armenian individuals or community, demanding so much money or provisions, the denial of which would always cost life, honor and property. Very often they would capture the sacred utensils of the church as a security for the payment of the demanded sum; or would take the abbot of the convent a prisoner and torture and disgrace him until the ransom was sent. When Christmas or Easter approached the chief of the town would send for the key of the

church, which the poor Christians could not dare to
refuse, and which they could hardly get back, even
by offering large sums of money and by begging for
months.   As to the janissaries (nominal soldiers in
the provinces), it is impossible to describe the horrible atrocities they have committed.   They at any
time, even late in the evening, would knock at the
gate of a well-to-do Armenian and demand the
immediate delivery of so much meat, rice, butter,
bread and wine, and sometimes worse.   The beys
and their subordinates and sub-subordinates, down to
the meanest servant would fall upon the helpless
Christians.   This was the general condition of the
Armenians during the first half of the present
century.

2.   **How Could the Armenians keep their Existence.**   In spite of so many disadvantages—religious,
political, local, external and internal—the Armenian
nation, though greatly reduced in number, has preserved its existence as a civilized Christian nation in
the East.   As to how—the chief points are already
mentioned in one of the preceeding chapters—it was
through their tenacity to the Christian religion, their
affinity to the fatherland, their natural abilities and
moral characteristics.   Other reasons which can be
mentioned in connection with this so-called feudal
system are as follows:

(*a*)   Every Christian family, or village, or district,
was identified by the name of a certain Turkish or
Kurdish aga or bey or sheikh.   When a Moslem met
an Armenian he would ask him, "What aga's giaour

are you?'' as one would say, ''Whose horse is
this?'' And the poor Christian, more intelligent
and less fortunate than a horse, was obliged to reply,
''I am ―― aga's giaour, sir,'' and would be dealt
with according to his relation with the said aga.
This tyrannical system of using the Christians as
private property and slaves, for the purchase and
support of which they paid nothing, would to some
extent protect the Armenians against public attacks,
but the main object of this system or protection was
for the only purpose of worrying them privately,
which may be illustrated by the following incident,
which is one of the many that occurred every day:

The greatest effendi (chief) of a certain town once
had heard that a certain Armenian bought a small
garden under the name of a subordinate Moslem,
whom he bribed to make this arrangement. The
said effendi sent for this Armenian, on whose arrival
the following conversation took place:

Effendi―''Chorbaji (soup-maker; wealthy Armenians are called by this title of honor), did you
hear that Allah gave us a new child in these days?''

Armenian―''Yes, your honor; may Allah grant
him long life.''

Eff.―''But, you know, it is the custom of our city
to give some present to new-born children.''

Arm.―(hesitatingly). ''Exactly, my lord; the
treasures of Egypt are worthy to be offered to your
son.''

Eff.―''Let us see what will your present be for
him.''

Arm.—"Your honor, I sacrifice my life for him; but, alas! what worthy present can be expected from a beggar like me!"

Eff.—"Hum! I heard all about it. You bought that field under the name of that rascal, eh?"

Arm.—"My lord, where shall the slave of your door find money enough to buy a field!"

Eff-—"Look here, Chorbaji, I am thinking only for your own good. Do you suppose that those wolves (other Turkish chiefs) will let you enjoy the benefit of your own property? Of course not. I'll tell you what to do. You better leave it to our new-born child as your present. Why will you buy calamity with your own money? If you need anything come to me."

It is not necessary to say that the garden referred to was then and there recorded to the name of the future tyrant now in the cradle.

(b) Armenians were obliged to hold the policy of concealment of their wealth, exceeding caution for their honor, and to be submissive. If they accumulated money, which, owing to their commercial ability and the Turks' and Kurds' stupidity, was an easy task, they were very careful not to let it be known, but put it in an earthen or copper vessel and buried it under the ground. In their clothing and houses they were very simple, so as not to attract attention. Women would wear the most common clothing when out of doors, and cover their ornaments under their robes. Not only for their property, but also for their honor and life they were very cautious. They would never travel alone unless some hired Kurd be with them. They would be very careful to close and lock their gates and doors early in the evening, and put strong iron bars and thick shutters to their small windows. They should always act and speak very kindly, even to the meanest Turk or Kurd, giving always the better side of the road to him, responding his salutation with bows or flattering words. If an Armenian was insulted or beaten or murdered by Kurds or Turks, his friends should keep silent in order not to add more horrors upon horrors. The constant counsel of the parents to their boys was not to go among the Moslem boys and not to return their bad conduct. There were streets, even quarters, in the towns where Christians could not dare to step. The women and the children were shut in their houses; the pretty girls were clothed like boys and wore short hair until their thirteenth year, when the poor creatures would be secretly married with another child in order to be saved from the assault of the brutes in human form. Thus skill, flattery, bribery and submission were the only means that Armenians could use for their benefit.

(c) *The Turks' and Kurds' own Benefit demanded the Armenians' Existence.* The Moslem is identified with his big turban around a very small and deformed head, wide coat, loose and heavy slippers, and a long pipe, sitting on his soft cushion, smoking lazily, and taking strong coffee frequently, walking very slowly, talking unintelligibly, giving his whole attention to his harem and kitchen, keeping a separate servant for each work in the house—one to look after the horses, and sometimes with subordinates under his command, one to prepare coffee, another to follow him and carry his four or five-foot-long pipe, one to tell hideous stories to entertain him and his guests, another to lead him in his five daily prayers, one to carry his child (on the shoulder, and teach him how to swear), one to oversee the crops, another to keep their record, and one to bring them in, etc.—ten, twenty or fifty, gathered in the house and in the harem depend upon him for their extravagant living. The endless flow of beggars, flatterers, fortune-tellers, good dreamers about the chief lady of the harem, guests, untimely callers and their horses, donkeys and camels—all these idle and gluttonous men and women cannot be supported by smoking in the corner of the house, or by hearing and telling stories about *houris* (the girls of paradise). There must be a constant source of supply. It is the poor Armenian's destiny to be the rayah, the pasture of this cursed flock. They are Turks' and Kurds' cornfields for eating, for selling, for trampling, and for burning. Who wants to give up such a support and laborers as the Armenians? It is true, occasionally they thin them out by the sword and reduce to poverty the remainder, but they are not so unwise as to exterminate them and be obliged to work themselves.

The Turk could not and can not exist without his non-Moslem subjects, and he is well aware of it.

CHAPTER XIII.

1. **The Origin of the Turks.** The Turks are supposed to be identical with the many and extensive Tartaric tribes scattered over the plains and table-lands of Central and Western Asia, pastoral in their occupations, warlike in disposition, plundering in habits, and nomadic in their mode of life. Their ancestors appear to have been known to the ancients by the general name of Scythians.

Like most other nationalities, the Turkish tribe have a legendary history which goes back to remote antiquity. They claim to be descended from an individual named Turk, a supposed grandson of Japheth. But their authentic history commences at a more recent date; for it was not till the fifth or sixth century, A. D., that Europe had any knowledge of the name and nation of the Turk. About that period, having migrated westward from Central Asia, the barren table-lands of Mongolia, they spread over the vast steppes now bearing the name of Turkestan.

In connection with the Armenian history the name of Seljouk Tartars or Turks are mentioned, in order to distinguish them from the Ottoman or Osmanli Turk, the present nation designated by that name. The reader is requested to remember that the Seljouks were first settled in Khorasan, the Persian province,

100

and founded an independent sovereignty that, under the three vigorous rulers Alp Arslan, Melik Shah and Togrul Bey, rapidly enlarged its bounds, as to include the whole of Persia, Armenia, Syria and the greater part of Asia Minor. The period of the Seljoukian kingdom in Asia Minor lasted about 250 years (1045-1299 A. D.). The Ottoman, or the present Turks, are their kindreds under a different dynasty or government, as will be seen elsewhere.

2. **The Conversion of the Turks to Mohametanism.** The religion of these Tartaric tribes, if they had any, seems to be very coarse heathenism; owing to their nomadic life and savage disposition they could not have fixed temples and systematic mode of worship, and regular religious organization of priesthood and teaching. In their semi-savage career, not much different from the wild animals, they did not show any sign of having been in contact with early Christianity, Hellenistic revival of letters and the European civilization; they had no literature or history until they met with the Saracens, the Mohametan warriors of Arabia, and were conquered and converted to Islam in Persia in the seventh century. Finding this new religion very suitable to their nature and habits they entered the service of the caliphs of Bagdad and swelled the Mohametan armies till the degenerate commander of the faithful (caliph of Bagdad) was compelled to resign his temporal power to the new converts, who pretended to respect the spiritual authority of the caliphate. Salur, the first Tartaric Mohametan chief of importance, called his tribe "Turk-iman," the Turks

of the Faith, to distinguish them from their brethren who continued in heathenism.

The Seljoukians, who were the descendents of Turkimans, and were called after the name of their leader Suljouk, established in Persia and surpassed the other Moslems of their age by fanaticism and fierce intolerance, and thereby provoked the famous crusades of the western Christian nations. After the fall of the Bagdad caliphate, Syria and Jerusalem fell into the hands of the Egyptian caliphate, but Seljouks, wresting Jerusalem for a time from the dominion of the latter, and dealing worse with the resident and pilgrim Christians, caused Europe to be armed for the deliverance of the oppressed,

3. **The rise of the Ottoman or Osmanli Turks.** At the death of Melik Shah, the Seljoukian sovereign, the unity of his vast dominions was ended in consequence of several candidates claiming the throne, and thus became divided into various principalities, until the irruption of the Mongols under the successors of Genghis Khan changed the entire political situation of the East and everywhere broke the power of the Seljouk Turks, and paved the way for the rise of their Ottoman successors, the present Turks.

About the middle of the thirteenth century another Turkish tribe, driven forward by the Mongol invaders, left their camping ground in Khorasan and wandered into Armenia in search of pasturage for their flocks. After seven years of exile, deeming the opportunity favorable to return, they set out to their ancient possessions; but while crossing the Euphrates the horse of their leader fell with him and he perished in the river. Upon this accident the tribe was divided into four companies by his sons, and Ertogrul, the warlike head of one division, resolved to turn back to the westward and seek a settlement in Asia Minor. While pursuing his course he saw two armies in hostile array, and joined himself to the apparently weaker party, and his timely aid decided the victory. The conquered were an invading horde of Mongols; the conqueror was Aladdin, the Seljouk Sultan of Iconium, one of the divided principalities of the great dominion of Melik Shah. As a reward of his timely help Aladdin assigned a territory for Ertogrul and his people, which consisted of the rich plains in the valley of the river Sangarius, and of the Black Mountains in Asia Minor. This was the accident which led to the establishment of the present Turkish empire, because Ertogrul was the ancestor of the present Ottoman dynasty.

4. **Osman the First (Ottoman) Turkish Sultan.** On the death of the Seljouk ruler of Iconium, who left no son to succeed him, the Emirs, the chiefs of the clans, divided his dominion into petty states among themselves. Osman, the son of Ertogrul, being one of these local chiefs, became practically an independent prince, 1289 A. D. His dominion as a Sultan began, however, in 1299, by the invasion of Nicomedia, the first conquest of the Ottoman Turks.

According to the native historians, a dream foretold to Osman his future greatness. While resting beneath the roof of a sheikh, whose daughter he admired, and whom he afterwards married, the sleeper fancied that he saw a tree sprouting from his own body, which grew rapidly in size and foliage till it covered with its branches the three continents of Europe, Asia and Africa. Beneath this tree four huge mountains raised their snowy tops, from the sides of which came four rivers, the Tigris, Euphrates, Danube and Nile. Through the avenues of the valleys were seen cities adorned with domes, towers and minarets; the crescent gleamed on every spire, and from every minaret was heard the voice of the muezzin, the Mohametan crier to worship, and these voices mingled with the notes of thousands of nightingales and other singing birds. Suddenly the branches and leaves of the tree assumed a glittering, sabre-like aspect, and moved by the breeze towards Constantinople. That capital of the world, placed at the junction of two seas and two continents, seemed like a precious diamond in a ring between two sapphires and emeralds. Osman was about to celebrate his marriage with the Byzantine city by placing the ring upon his finger when he awoke.

5. **Janissaries, the Furious Turkish Soldiers.** Owing to the decayed condition of the Byzantine (Greek) empire, the Turks marched westward, and beginning with Nicomedia, gradually enlarged their dominion. In the year 1354 they crossed the strait of Dardanelles and set foot upon the soil of Europe. This was the first invasion any Tartaric or Turkish sovereign gained over this continent, and was also a preparation for the capture of Constantinople. This occurred at the time of Sultan Orchan's reign.

By this time the necessity of a permanent military force was felt, and the grand vizier, the prime minister of the Sultan, established a corps of infantry, who, not having yet forgotten, however, the pastoral life, proved ungovernable and unfit for the strict discipline of military life.   To remove this difficulty he resorted to rearing up in the doctrine of Islam the children of the conquered Christians, training them from early youth to the profession of arms, and forming them into a separate corps called "Yeni Cheri" (janissary), the new troops.

The corps proved very valiant, and continued to be supplied by the children of captives taken in war, or by those of Christian subjects.   An inhuman tax of every fifth child, or of one child every fifth year, was strictly levied upon them.   It has been estimated that not less than half a million Christian children thus cruelly torn from their parents, were made Moslems, and trained them to maintain Islam with the sword.   Afterwards the children of janissaries themselves were admitted into regiments, thus they became a military class, distinguished by their fanaticism in religion, bravery in wars and cruelty against Christians.   Through upwards of three centuries, marked by a long series of great battles, they sustained only four signal reverses.   Victory and despotic rule marched hand in hand under their banner; but by the gradual advance of the European nations their power failed abroad, while their disorder increased at home and they became formidable to their masters, deposing them from the throne and raising to it, till, unable otherwise to suppress their boldness, Sultan Mahmoud II., the grandfather of the present Sultan, had the entire order exterminated by the sword.

CHAPTER XIV.

THE CAPTURE OF CONSTANTINOPLE.

In order to show the effect of this great historical event upon European civilization, and to illustrate the style of Turkish invasions, it is worth while to say something on this subject.

1. **The Capture of Constantinople.** According to the established usage of the education of the Turkish princes, Sultan Mohamet was placed under the care of fanatic tutors, so that Islam in all its fierceness and bigotry early enslaved his mind, and he grew up a strict observer of its rites and spirit; for he is said never to have conversed with a Christian without afterwards purifying himself by the legal mode of ablution. Having twice been clothed with the regal dignity, and twice suspended in the lifetime of his father, Mohamet finally gained possession of it when twenty years of age. He may be called the most gifted of all the sultans, but he certainly was one of the most detestable. He commenced his reign with the murder of his younger brothers, who were destroyed to make the throne an indisputable possession. From the moment of his accession all his thoughts were directed to give the death-blow to the Greek empire, and to transfer the seat of his government to Constantinople. Adrianople was the Turkish capital by this time.

2. **Preliminary Steps Toward the Siege of Constantinople.** On the European side of the Bosphorus, about five miles above the city proper, Sultan Mohamet raised a fortress opposite to one on the Asiatic side, which had been erected by one of his predecessors. The Greek Emperor, Constantine Palæologus, heard of the rise of the massive towers in his neighborhood with alarm; and his anxiety increased upon quarrels arising between his subjects and the Turkish workmen. The latter invaded without scruple the surrounding villages and despoiled homes; horses and mules were turned into the tilled fields and the crops destroyed. If resistance was offered, insult was repeated in an aggravated form. Constantine implored the Sultan to observe the courtesies of peace, till, convinced of his hostile intentions, he closed the gates of the capital and prepared himself for the inevitable approach of open war. "My trust," said he, "is in God alone; if it should please him to soften your heart, I shall rejoice in the happy change; if he delivers my city into your hands I shall submit without a murmur. But until the Judge of the whole earth pronounces between us, it is my duty to live and die in defense of my people." In the autumn of that year (1452) Mohamet withdrew to Adrianople, after carefully viewing the grounds about the city and examining its defenses. "Next summer," he said, "I must take up my abode in Constantinople." Both parties during the winter prepared for the approaching struggle.

3. **The Siege of the City.** Having collected his resources early in the spring of 1453, Mohamet enclosed the city with an army of 120,000 men, desolated the environs and confined the inhabitants within the walls. Engines of war and guns of great magnitude were slowly dragged by oxen from Adrianople. One huge piece of artillery is particularly noticed, which had a caliber of twelve spans in diameter, and could carry a stone ball of 600 pounds over a mile. But the imperfect condition of it was indicated by the circumstance that it could be loaded and fired only seven times in one day. It finally bursted with an awful explosion, killing the gunner and others. Including army and navy, the total force brought against the city was 260,000 strong. On the other side was a garrison of only 8,000 soldiers, who had to defend a circuit of thirteen miles, comprising both sea and land.

In the Turkish army sheikhs and fanatics predicted a triumph and repeated the dream of Osman from tent to tent, and the passages from Koran was quoted as expressly promising this conquest: "Know ye a city encompassed on two sides by water and on the third by land; the last hour shall not come before it be taken by 60,000 of the faithful." The Greeks, few in number but brave in spirit, heroically defended their walls and kept the enemy in check for more than fifty anxious days. So powerful was their resistance that Mohamet at one time despaired of success and thought of raising the siege, but overwhelming numbers proved irresistible in the final assault.

The Sultan prepared for it characteristically on the preceding day by a religious festival, which involved a rigid fast, ablution seven times repeated, the prayer for victory, and a general illumination. As the night approached lamps were hung out before every tent and fires were kindled in various localities. Thousands of lanterns were suspended from the flag-staffs of the batteries and from the masts and yards of the ships, but a deep silence prevailed through the entire camp. The meaning of these demonstrations without the walls was truly interpreted by those within. Emperor and subjects, bishops and priests, monks and nuns, men, women and children, formed processions to the churches, singing supplicatory chants by the way, with the accompaniment of "the holy and venerable images and the divine pictures." Constantine went that night to St. Sophia and received the sacrament.

4. **The Fall of the City.** Before dawn on the fatal day the signal was given for the attack, and it was obeyed with greatest delight. Column after column advanced in orderly array.. For two hours the besieged kept the enemy at bay. Then the Greek commander received a wound which. unnerved him, and dispirited by this calamity the defenders' courage failed them, while that of the foe increased. Led by an officer called Hassan, a company of janissaries crossed the ruins in the ditch, gained the breach and mastered the position. Constantine fell in defending it; Hassan, too, was slain; and over the bodies of both the Turks rushed into Constanti-

nople. . The terrified Greek population hastened into the sanctuary of St. Sophia for protection, and to the last moment many clung to the belief that an angel would be sent from heaven there to vindicate the orthodoxy of the Greek church and destroy the Mohametan who should dare to enter its door. The victor, attended by his pashas and generals, visited the desolate hall of the imperial palace, and arriving at the door of St. Sophia alighted from his horse, passed into the temple, and ordered all the crosses to be thrown down and all the paintings torn from the walls, and got upon his knees and muttered his prayer. A few days afterwards the muezzin proclaimed the public invitation for prayer in the name of Allah and His apostle, Mohamet. Thus the stately edifice of Justinian, which upon its completion drew from him the exclamation, "I have outdone thee, O Solomon," became a Mohametan mosque, and has ever since been preserved with the greatest care and pride.

After a time of perfect license to his ferocious troops, the Sultan undertook the task of repairing the ravages of war, and commemorated his triumph by taking the proud title of "The Lord of Two Continents and Two Seas," and fixed his residence on the site of the imperial palace, and founded that seraglio where his successors have resided, and which has been the scene of so much luxury, violence and crime.

5. "Lord, **Save Us from the Devil, the Turk and the Comet.**" It was the settled purpose of Mohamet II. to extend his empire to the west, and some succeeding sultans also entertained the same idea;

and for over a century after the capital of Christendom in the east surrendered, the liberties and institutions of the western nations were seriously threatened. In the year 1456 a comet passed very near the orbit of the earth, and swept the heavens with a tail extending over 60 degrees, in the form of a sword or saber.   Men watched it with mingled emotions at Rome, Vienna and Constantinople. - The night of the full moon having come, and then by chance an eclipse having taken place at the latter city, some thought that the Christian inhabitants of the west had agreed to march against the Turks, and would gain the victory.   The Pope, however, regarded the comet as in league with the Moslems, and ordered the prayer "Ave Maria" to be repeated three times a day instead of twice.   He directed the church bells to be tolled at noon, a custom which still prevails in Roman Catholic countries.   To the "Ave Maria" the prayer was added, "Lord, save us from the devil, the Turk and the comet."   Every first Sunday of the month a solemn procession was appointed, with a special mass, and a sermon upon the subject. The comet at length, after patiently enduring some months of daily excommunication, showed signs of retreat, and Europe breathed more freely when it vanished from the skies.

CHAPTER XV.

1. **Diversions of the Designs of Turkish Ambition.** Four centuries ago the powers of Europe were summoned to solemn meetings to take counsel for the expulsion of the Turk from Europe, but they could not come to an agreement before some internal events turned the Turkish ambition from the west to the east, from the shores of the Adriatic to the defiles of Armenia, and from the banks of the Danube to the plains of Egypt.

The reign of Sultan Bayazit, the son and successor of Mohamet the conqueror of Constantinople, was greatly disturbed by the rebellion of his brother, who effectually contended for the throne. After a long civil war, being driven to extremity, the prince placed himself under the protection of the Knights of Rhodes, who sent him to France, from whence he was sent to Italy and kept as a prisoner of State in the Vatican. He there served as a hostage for the good conduct of the Sultan, since, in case the latter should become aggressive toward the Christian nations, the captive might be let loose against him as a competitor.

The janissaries, on the other hand, haughty and powerful, were a constant cause of anxiety to the Sultan, and even bribes failed to keep them in subjection to their unfavored master. They made the

113

revolt of his youngest son Selim a success, not only in forcing Bayazit to abdicate and leave the capital, but hastening his death while yet on the road to his place of exile.   The military spirit and ability of the new Sultan made him a favorite with the janissaries, while his religious frenzy and severity rendered him acceptable to the more bigoted Moslems.

2.   **Possession of the Islamic Caliphate.**   Soon after getting to the throne Sultan Selim, surnamed Cruel, turned his armies eastward, and after reducing Armenia and Mesopotamia conducted a successful war in Persia against Shah Ismael, another Mohametan ruler in the east.   Persians and Turks, both of the same faith, had a severe religious dispute among themselves in regard to the legitimacy of the first three caliphs, the successors of the Prophet Mohamet. The Persian Moslem rejected them as usurpers, and began to count the true succession with the fourth caliph, Ali, the son-in-law of the prophet.   On entering upon his eastern campaign Sultan Selim proclaimed it to be a religious war, and the legal decree of the Turkish mufties ''that there was more religious merit in killing one Persian than in shedding the blood of seventy Christians,'' strengthened the Turkish fanaticism against their co-religionists.

The fiery Sultan, at the head of a victorious army, next invaded Syria and Egypt, and added those vast and valuable territories to his possessions.   The conqueror showed his bloody disposition the day after the surrender of Cairo by causing the Egyptian governor to be executed at one of its gates and the

30,000 captives slaughtered in his presence and thrown into the Nile. El Mutevekkil, the last Mohametan caliph in Egypt, was deposed from his rank as the spiritual head of Islam and the Turkish Sultan was clothed with the dignity by the sheriff of Mecca, who consigned the keys of the Kabeh to his hand. Sultan Selim consequently added to his other titles that of "the Caliph of Moslems, and the Shadow of Allah Upon the Earth, and the Defender of the Two Holy Cities (Mecca and Medina)." After this victory he returned to Constantinople with the plunder of Egypt, which required a train of a thousand camels to carry. His successors have since been regarded as the supreme chief of the Moslem world and the Commander of the Faithful.

3. **The Turks at the Gate of Vienna.** The reign of Sultan Soliman (1520–1566) was the most memorable in the history of the empire when it reached its climax, which was never afterwards surpassed. Three years after the conquest of Belgrade and Rhodes the first French Ambassador appeared at the Turkish Court. The envoy came apparently to negotiate a general commercial treaty, but really to procure a powerful ally for his master Francis I. against the German Emperor Charles V. The division of Christendom into Romanism and Protestantism had commenced, and the anxiety to gain predominance led the unwise monarchs to avail themselves of the services of this mighty Mohametan State.

Sultan Soliman, according to his word with the French king to carry a campaign beyond the Danube and divert the attention and the arms of the Austrian house, crossed the said river at the head of 100,000 men with 300 pieces of artillery. The day after the terrible "Destruction of Mahoc" in Hungary the Sultan received in state the compliments of his officers, when the heads of 2,000 of the slain, including those of seven bishops, were piled up as a trophy before his pavilion. At the approach of winter Soliman returned to Constantinople laden with booty and many captives, leaving an impoverished and de-populated country to be contended for by rival pretenders to the throne.

The next summer the Turkish army, upwards of 200,000 strong, advanced in the direction of Vienna, capturing castles and towns and devasting the country, till from the walls of the Austrian capital the gloomy light of burning villages were seen round half the horizon. The Turks reached Vienna and the siege immediately commenced, but notwithstanding the numerical inferiority of the garrison they were repulsed at every assault and suffered severely from the sallies. Being discouraged, the Turks prepared for an effective and last attack, the walls around the city and all breaches were re-examined by the Sultan and his grand vizier, and immense sums of money were distributed among the soldiers. Enthused by these means a general assault was ordered on the 14th day of October, 1529, but such was the desperate valor of the defenders that the Turks were foiled in every effort. Owing to the advance of the season and the absence of provisions the troops were discontent and it became necessary to raise the siege.

4. Greatest Extent of the Empire. The Ottoman Turks, once a petty tribe of unsettled wanderers, without an acre of soil they could call their own, had now become, in little more than three centuries, great among the European nations, occasionally endangering their independence, civilization and religion. They possessed the most favored climate of the earth and the most fertile soil; a seaboard abounding in convenient roads and harbors; an archipelago offering facilities to commerce; straits the most impassable to him who has not the key or who is not on friendly terms with the owner, and a capital adapted by its geographical position to become the center of a dominion extending to three continents. They were masters of countries the most interesting from their sacred, classic and historical associations; the scenes where patriarchs pitched their tents and prophets delivered their oracles, and the soil on which the Savior of the World was born and where apostles first proclaimed the gospel of salvation.

Their empire included in Europe Roumelia, Bulgaria, Servia, Bosnia, Montenegro, Thessalia, Greece and greater part of Hungary; in Asia all Asia Minor, Armenia, Georgia, Daghistan, Kurdistan, Mesopotamia, Syria, Cyprus and the chief part of Arabia; in Africa Egypt, Tripoli, Tunis and Algiers; while the khanate of Crimea, the principalities of Valachia and Moldavia and Transylvania, with the republic of Raguza, were vassal states. Also diplomatic and commercial relations subsisted between the Porte and the leading powers of Christendom.

5. **Decline and Its Causes.** Though the Turks benefited by the political disadvantages of the surrounding nations, and encouraged by the mutual jealousy and selfishness of the so-called Christian powers had made themselves a name and built up a colossal power, they were destitute of the qualities which alone give honor to greatness and can secure permanence to success. The discipline of the seraglio (Turkish palace) was fatal to a succession of able rulers. The princes of blood, confined within its walls and separated from general society, deprived of every honorable ambition, with eunuchs for their teachers and slaves for their companions, resigned themselves to guilty pleasures to dissipate the tedium of such an existence, and were only fitted, if raised to the throne, to act the part of timid puppets or unmanly tyrants.

The genius of Mohametanism, by the vain claims of superiority and its stern fatalism, contributed much to retain the Turks in a stationary condition, which necessarily became one of increasing inferiority in comparison with the other nations of Europe. Educated in a creed which confines the intellect to the Koran and inspires sovereign contempt for nations, arts and institutions without the pale of Islam, resigned to the belief that all events happen by inevitable necessity, an arrest was laid upon intellectual cultivation.

The essentially military constitution of the empire also insured its decay. History continually repeats the lesson that power founded by the sword and depending merely upon the sword for its maintenance can never be firm and permanent. The Turks were formidable so long as they could reap a harvest of plunder from the states and countries around them, but when a stop was put to their career of conquest by the increased power of their neighbors and they had to act upon the defensive the deficiency of their own resources was soon apparent, and would ere this have been blotted irreparably from the list of European kingdoms but for the intervention of selfish interests.

CHAPTER XVI.

1. **The Nature of the Turkish Government.** The Turkish Government is what we may call a politico-religious system. The Sultan claims to be the successor of the prophet, hence the highest authority over the Mohametan world. The Turkish army is exclusively a Mohametan army. All the struggles and wars, however political they may be, are regarded and fought as religious wars, always sanctioned by the legal decree from the highest religious authority, and led by " sanjak- sherif," the holy banner of the " Apostle of Allah," used in religious contests of the Saracens. The law of the Turkish courts in its essentials and details is based upon the Koran, administered and executed by Mohametan judges, who are the white-turbaned religious heads of the community. In one word, the interest of the Turkish Government is that, and only that, of Islam. Hence the more zealous and intolerant a sultan the nearer the ideal of a Mohametan ruler, and more respected and obeyed by the bigoted people, officers and the army.

Another phase of the Turkish Government is its dualism. It is a government within a government. Two words, porte and palace, express these elements. The whole machinery of government exists at the porte, Council of Ministers and Council of State. All business is supposed to pass through their hands, and the whole administration subordinates to them; still all being subject to the supreme will of the Sultan. Any decision issued from the porte must be carried by the grand vizier to "the foot of the throne" and the Sultan's arbitrary utterance in positive or negative must be regarded as a "firman," the command of "God's shadow upon the earth." The palace is another center of authority more powerful than the official government, made up of chamberlains, mollahs, eunuchs, astrologers and nondescripts, and supported by the secret police. The general policy of the empire is determined by this party, and the most vital questions of the State are often treated and decided here, while the highest officials of the porte are left in absolute ignorance of what is going on. This party (palace), composed of the representatives of the most fanatic Moslems and the meanest adventurers, native or foreign, have the greatest influence upon the will and deeds of the Sultan. Not a single communication passes to or from the Sultan but by their agency, and with frequent modification or total fabrication.

2. **The Government and the Christian Subjects.** The inhabitants of Turkey, consisting of about fifteen different races or nationalities, are, in the sight of the government and law, divided into two essential classes under the official names of "Moslem" and "non-Moslem." Turks, Arabs, Kurds, Albanians, Tartars, Circassians and Africans belong to the

"blessed" class (Moslem), while the Armenians, Greeks, Nestorians, Maronites, Jews, Druzes and Europeans belong to the condemned party (non-Moslem).

Being led by the necessities of affairs, and often enforced by the commanding requests of the European Powers, the Turkish sultans apparently adopted and even officially proclaimed some religious and civil reforms for their non-Moslem subjects; but these schemes of toleration did not go further than the waste-basket. Sultan Mohamet II., the capturer of Constántinople, seeing that the population of the great capital had been thinned out by the sword, by flight and captivity, issued a general proclamation assuring the Greeks who chose to become settlers " that they would be protected in their lives and lib erties, in the free exercise of their religion, enjoying certain privileges relative to their commercial pursuits; that they were to elect their own patriarchs, subject to approval of the supreme power and were to enjoy the same honors and ranks that had belonged to their predecessors in the ecclesiastical office," etc.; while another sultan, the grandfather of the present one, being informed of the existence of a conspiracy among the Greek subjects abroad, gave way to frantic ráge and let loose the passion of his Moslem subjects against the Greek Christians in the capital and the provinces. Thousands of innocent victims were sacrificed to their vengeance, many of them without even knowing why they were slain. On Easter day the Gregorian patriarch of Constantinople was executed at the door of his own church, and as the greatest possible indignity which could be offered in the eyes of his nation his body was delivered to the Jews to be dragged through the streets. This was what "the honors and ranks" of the above quoted proclamation meant and as understood by the sultans.

" *The Hatti Sheriff*," sacred document " of Gulhane," promulgated by Sultan Mejit, the father of the present Sultan, as a concession of " equal rights and justice to all classes of the Ottoman subjects," infuriated the bitter feelings of the fanatical Turks, who, unable to bear the idea of being placed on the same level with the "infidel dogs," excited the ignorant population in the capital and provinces and imposed insults and outrages upon the Christians.

The 61st article of the Treaty of Berlin (1878), signed by the Turk, together with the six great Powers of Europe, to bring an end to the Kurdish and Circassian atrocities committed in Armenia, resulted in the Sassoun massacre of 1894, and the last issue of the scheme of reforms signed by the Sultan and published in eight columns of London papers caused the slaughter of 80,000 innocent Armenians with such horrors that 800 pages of the same papers could not describe and eighty centuries will not be able to wipe away this unparalleled blot on the eighteen Christian governments of Europe.

3. **Constitutional Privileges of the Armenian Church.** Nearly thirty-five years ago, after repeated appeals and great struggles, the Armenian mother church secured a constitution granted by the Sultan

pertaining to her ecclesiastical rights as to the election and privileges of the patriarchs and synods and provincial councils, and the administration of the schools and other institutions. This constitution, though carefully sifted and limited by Turkish severity, was once supposed to be the guarantee for the protection of the ecclesiastical rights so long disregarded, but soon proved to be a farce upon the part of the Turkish Government. From the election of the patriarch, the head of the executive body of the said constitution and the only authorized agent between the Armenian church and the Turkish government, to the appointment of the village teacher, every transaction was meddled with, disturbed, delayed, and frequently prevented by the "good pleasure of the all-powerful Padishah" (the monarch), as well as by the least and the meanest clerk of the porte.

In 1850 the Protestant Armenians were granted a charter guaranteeing them "religious liberty and other rights conferred on the other Christian communities of the empire." In spite of these promises they have never been allowed to erect one church in the capital, though they have the site and the necessary funds in hand and have repeatedly petitioned for the same during fifteen successive years.

The Catholic Armenians, having their own so-called patriarch in Constantinople, and being indirectly helped by the Roman church, have comparatively greater access to the palace, and that by the cunning policy of the Tur ish government, in order to sow tares among the Christian communities of the empire.

In official documents these three branches of the Armenian church are intentionally distinguished by the names of "the Protestant nation," "the Catholic nation" and "the Armenian nation" (the old church). And the common people, unable to realize the real spirit of this distinction, receive it as a compliment and recognition of their equal rights.

4. Governmental Offices for non-Moslems. Non-Moslems are entirely left out of the legal and military services. No Christian is admitted in the Turkish army or navy as a soldier; some few Greeks and Armenians, however, serve as physicians in the army.

According to the later constitution, each community in the empire should have their representatives at the courts in proportion to the numbers of Moslems and and non-Moslems of the country (not of the respective towns), as one to four; the president being always a Moslem and each Christian member being approved by the government herself. Under such limitations there could not be much room for the protection of Christians' rights, especially in the interior, where the Turkish members arrange matters and prepare reports to suit themselves and offer them to the Christian members to sign, even without reading the contents, and that most probably at the expense of the rights of their own friends and communities. Fear, ignorance, and sometimes selfish interests, compel them to do so.

Coming to other subordinate offices, as in telegraphic or postal departments, or in financial or register bureaus, etc., the Christians are used as

helpers or chief laborers for the higher Moslem
officers, who are either unable or unwilling to work
and are glad to use such active and honest brains and
hands for one third of the assigned salary.

CHAPTER XVII.

TURKISH TAXES AND THE MODE OF COLLECTING.

If the institution of government is based upon the idea of justice, protection and mutual help for human progress, the Turkish rule has no right to claim that title. One of the most evident reasons of this accusation is her tax system, which is nothing less than a highway robbery, a well organized system to suck the last drop of blood from the veins of her subjects, be they Moslems or non-Moslems.

The following taxes and the mode of collection will explain the existing affairs in that country:

1. **Taxes on Real Estate.** This is about three per cent of the entire value of the property, to be paid every year, the value being determined by the government. The severity of this tax and degradation attached to its collection is more keenly felt in the interior of the empire, especially in small towns and farm villages. There comes a company of ruffians under the title of "Padishah Zabtiehsy" (king's police), numbering five, seven or more, armed to the teeth, tough, ignorant, vulgar and gluttonous men, who stop at the house of the wealthiest, call the leading men of the community and having stated the amount demanded of the town, threaten them in the name and by the authority of the Sultan, "the Father of the Faithful, whose mercy and wisdom fill the

127

earth." These fiends, known as collectors, live on the people for one, two or more weeks, demanding the best of provisions, dictating the bill of fare themselves. Their horses also must be taken good care of by the town, even if it takes the tender gardens or the fields. Among the means employed by these collectors are beating men with many stripes, smearing the face with cow's manure, tying men to the tree or the wall, head fixed and the eyelids stretched up and down so as to expose the eyes to the burning sun for hours at a time, have the body bent forward, place a heavy rock or log on the back until the muscles and joints give way and sometimes the blood gushes from the nose, and many other such things. The violation of personal honor and unspeakable deeds imposed upon men and women must pass silently. These deeds continue day after day with increased intensity until the community is compelled to sell everything at any price to get rid of such brave and faithful officers of "His Imperial Majesty, whose goodness spreads all over the world."

These atrocities are imposed not upon the Christians alone, but upon the Moslems also. Still the injustice practiced upon the former is immeasurably severe. In a village known to the writer the total amount demanded for the year was 39,000 piasters, of this 33,465 piasters were paid by 180 Christian families, while twice as many Turkish families paid only 5,535 piasters.

2. **Taxes on Agricultural Products.** The vineyards, orchards, gardens and grain fields compose

this class. The rate levied upon the products is nominally one-eighth, but the time of determining the value and the mode of collecting brings it as high as one-fourth or more. The fruit products are valued by the collectors and while yet in blossom, and though the crops may fail, still the taxes must be paid. It often occurs that vineyards and orchards are deserted by their owners in order to get rid of the heavy taxes. The right of collecting "the tithes" on wheat and similar products is sold to parties known as tithers, most cruel and heartless men, and a great terror to the farmers. The tithes are de- manded for the simple fact that the ground, though bought with the money of its owner, is regarded as the absolute property of the government; therefore, the former must pay for the privilege of using the ground. According to this principle one cannot turn his own field into a garden or orchard, nor can he build houses upon it, nor even can he sell it, without the official permission of the government. The law is that if a field is not tilled for three successive years the government has the right to confiscate it and sell it to others. Because of the absence of modern machinery and many obstacles in the way, an average farmer can cultivate but ten or twelve acres of land. After hard labor and constant watch over the field from the tenderest growth to the harvest, the farmer is not allowed to use any part of the products until the tither has measured the crop and taken his part. So soon as the threshing is over an agent of the tither puts his stamp all around and over the piles of the wheat and orders the farmer to watch and wait until he comes again to measure it. In the meantime the farmer has no bread to eat and no oats for his stock, and is obliged to borrow at a rate of fifty per cent interest. He may have to wait for weeks and sometimes until late in the autumn watching over his crop day and night to keep off the cattle and robbers from disturbing "the marks," in which case he will be accused of stealing and must lose more. When the farmers of the town send word and beg the tithers to come and settle the business the rude answer is "Yavash, Yavash" (slowly, slowly). When they do come a horror fills the town, farmers are accused of stealing, insulted, beaten and condemned for so much damage, the act and the mode of execution being in their own hands. After the alleged damages are rectified in their own fashion, the turn comes to the "legal tithe, the divine right bestowed upon the Sultan, the successor to the prophet." From the best portion of the crop the right of the government is secured.

3. **Taxes on Herds and Flocks.** The tax levied upon each sheep, etc., is estimated about one-eighth of the entire value due in the spring, when the sheep sell for the least money. As a hard winter passes, when the owner of the flock has consumed all provisions and left nothing to pay this tax, he is obliged to sell a part of his flock for only one-third of the price they could easily get in the autumn. The only reason this tax is demanded in the spring is because the number of the sheep and goats are greatest at that time.

4. **Haraj** or **Zimmet**. This tax, demanded of non-Moslems only, is a religious tribute, which according to the Koran, giaours have to pay for their existence and their "infidel religious rights." According to this doctrine no Christian subject can be allowed to live under the Mohametan dominion without humbly surrendering to this demand. Under the Turkish rule, which is the best representative of the Mohametan institution, this tax is nominally contrasted with the military service of the Moslem subjects, from which the Christians are "exempt," or rather, deprived. This is an annual tax imposed upon every male member of the non-Moslem communities at the rate of two dollars each, and in advance. The Turkish Government believes strictly in cash business with her own subjects, leaving all delays for her transactions with the foreigners. This tax the government is very severe and prompt to collect. The poor who are not able to pay at the demanded time are insulted, imprisoned, beaten and even tortured in the most brutal manner, mentioned under the head of "The Turkish Prisons." Their property, houses, cattle, tools, even bedding and common utensils, are forcibly sold, the buyers being mostly Mohametans or the officers themselves. This tax begins at birth and goes through life. Often the tributes of the dead are collected from their relatives or churches for several years after their death until a new census is taken. Many persons unable to pay try to conceal themselves from the sight of the collector, give up their work, and sometimes their home, for a temorary relief at least,

5. **Taxes on Trade.** Every man except the farmer is expected to follow a trade, hence a tax levied on all above fifteen years of age, increasing as the age advances. The supposed gain on a given trade is determined by the authorities, and three to four per cent. demanded whether the person follows his trade during the year or not; hard times and failure in business excuse no one.

Besides the above taxes there are various fees and dues—duty on merchandise, fees on birth and marriage and death and burial; dues on building, repairing, planting and change of residence; dues on traveling, buying and selling. Great amounts of money are often collected for the "improvement of the roads and erection of public buildings and bridges, but no one can see where such roads and buildings are or ask questions about them without being accused of rebellion, which means imprisonment, torture and loss. Frequently a general announcement is circulated all over the country declaring urgent needs of the government and demanding immediate response for this "obligatory help," as it is called. Well-to-do persons, especially among the Christians, are forced to share in this involuntary virtue.

CHAPTER XVIII.

THE ABUSES IN TURKISH RULE.

Here lies one of the curses of Turkish Government. Many things are tolerably good on paper, but the actual practice never harmonizes with the written law in Turkey. The ignorance and unworthiness of the officers may be one of the reasons of this misery, but the greatest defect lies in their principle and character.

1. Bribery. The majority of the offices are merely sold to those who bid the highest. A cadi (judge), for example, cannot stay in the same country more than twenty-seven months at one time, during which period he gets about $1,000 for his whole service. No cadi can have a position without first paying to the higher authorities at Constantinople an average sum of $800, sometimes as much as his whole salary. This mutual agreement upon bribery and unjust taxation is understood in all departments of the government and the nominations settled accordingly. Offices are bought and services, just or unjust, are sold for the highest price.

Every officer has a nominal salary, yet many weeks and months may pass during which they cannot receive a single payment; yet they all keep their places, live luxuriously, accumulate wealth and never fail to pray for the prosperity of "the Sultan, the crown-giver of the princes of the world," under whose protection the wolves are set loose upon the lambs.

No man expects to transact business or receive attention in a Turkish court without bribery. The well-known Turkish proverb is that, " As soon as the bribery enters the door the justice escapes from the window." The doors and the windows of Turkish courts are kept open day and night for this accursed draft.

In a great many instances the bribery is practiced at the expense of the central government. The merchants save more by having goods pass through this bribery channel than by the ordinary way. A few meji- dichs (dollars) given to an officer or two under the name of "bakshish" (present), will save $40 to $50. Many forbidden books and papers enter the country and circulate widely through bribery. Many build- ings and repairs are allowed through the same means. In fact, if the officers would regard the law and the orders more than bribery, 50 per cent. of the trans- actions in various lines of business would be impos- sible, especially for the Christians. It is the opinion of the writer that bribery, though detrimental to the interests of the central government, is the only good thing in the whole machinery of the corrupt rule. The Sultan's government has for several years posi- tively forbidden the granting of pass-ports to Christians for foreign ports, with repeated orders for arrest and imprisonment of those who allow them to pass; yet bribery has kept the ports open for those who could afford to pay from $3 to $300.

2. **The Robbery by the Sultan's Officers.** The most important question in the mind of every officer is not the welfare of the government or of the people, but to devise a new plan to draw more money for themselves regardless of the mode or the consequences. Pasha Effendi (the governor) plans with kaimakam beys (the mayors) to blackmail some wealthy Armenian, or Greek or Jewish merchant, which never fails in resulting a goodly sum for our guardian of justice.

The police department is evidently known as the partner of thieves and the president of the societies of highwaymen. If you have some property stolen and feel anxious to get it back, make a skillful application to the chief of the police and pay something, say half the price of your loss, "as the governmental expenses for the search in the town and the expedition about," and you will be sure nine in ten to succeed.

The zaptiehs go from khan to khan (Turkish hotel) and seize the strangers or travelers and inquire about their regular license of trade. If they are able to show it they are asked to present the official receipt of the payment of the current year. If they do this they are demanded to show that of the last year, and if they can do so then are required to prove they are the persons they call themselves. When that is done the officer takes a paper out of his pocket and says: "You are to be arrested and sent to such a place. Here, I have the order (giving your description), 'dark hair, medium size and round face;' you are the man I was after for three weeks, and during this period a dozen telegrams were received about you. Get up, now, you dog giaour! You are a member of those secret societies which are plotting against the highest wealth '' (government). By this time the whip is at work, and it will not stop unless one mejidieh or two is slipped into the officer's hand.

At the custom house the goods are roughly handled and spoiled. Photographic plates and drugs are exposed to light with the excuse of ascertaining whether there be any dynamite concealed in the case. Many watches, jewels, fountain pens, etc., find their way to the examiner's pockets, their empty cases being put back honestly in their original places. The eatables are freely consumed by the officers and sometimes carried to their dinner tables at home.

The government itself is robbed by its own officers. In one of the provinces the government had a bridge built at a certain town. The architect of the said bridge, an Armenian or a Greek, brought the bill of expenditure, which was 8,000 piasters. The mayor looked over it and with great anger tore it in pieces, to the surprise and terror of the architect, who was ordered to be taken to the prison. After some days a sub-officer came to the jail and talked with the architect and informed him confidentially about the secret of the mayor's indignation and the way to appease it. Soon another bill was prepared for 20,-000 piasters, and everything was all right with the architect. The city clerk who recorded this sum had in the course of several years a position in the finance department at the capital, and saw one day that the same amount had been raised to 80,000 piasters before it reached there. This is but an illustration of daily and universal practice of the Turkish officers.

3. **Delay.** Delay is one of the proverbial characteristics of the Turkish rule. The words "yavash, yavash" (slowly, slowly), and "gelen hafta" (next week), are the constant utterance and the habitual motto of every officer throughout the empire. The Occidentals, though aware of the Turks' "deceit and delay," have not yet fully realized its depth. The crafty sultans played wonderful tricks in deceiving the European governments with their mysterious "yavashes," and the Government of the United States may keep receiving the same endless answer to its mild claims of indemnity for the mission properties destroyed by the soldiers of the Sultan. The Turks' "next week" will never come unless the language of gunpowder is used by Uncle Sam, as that is the only language the unspeakable Turk understands.

Electricity, so swift in its traveling throughout Europe and America, seemingly has lost its nature in Turkey. A message sent by telegraph to a distance of only twenty or thirty miles sometimes takes one or two days to reach its destination. The postal service is an eminent specimen of the Turkish promptness in business. The cities of 20,000 or 50,000 inhabitants receive mail but once a week, if they receive any, and that on the condition of entirely fair weather. The mail may arrive late in the afternoon simply because the drivers stopped for some rest in a coffee-house on the route, and the policy of "yavash, yavash," detained them for several hours; and when they reach the city in the afternoon, say three or four o'clock, the officials put the mail bags away for the next morning and the anxious waiters (mostly merchants) are sent back because the post-master declares "ajeleh yock; yavash, yavash" (there is no hurry; slowly, slowly). The writer once received mail four days after its arrival in the city. Registered letters are delivered later than the others as a rule.

On the ordinary business days the members of the Turkish court come late and irregular. The ice cream sellers are always ready at the hall of the court in hot weather and the coffee pot is there in the winter. The shoemaker comes at the office hour to get the measure of the cadi's foot; the tailor comes to fit the coat of the chief clerk. Soon a dervish enters the courtyard and begins his work of singing, as "Padi-shah does not lodge in a palace unless it is well finished; no man can reach to the truth unless he is far from the world." Before he has finished his verses a mob may rush in dragging a Jew or a Chris-tian who is accused of having cursed a mollah's turban or Mohamet's tomb, which may cause such an uproar as to consume the whole day and cost much money to the falsely accused giaour.

Fridays and Sundays, the two weekly holidays, are the best pretexts to put the engagements off. If Ramazan (the fasting month) is near you can not expect anything done this side of Bairam (great festival at the end of Ramazan). If the governor of the province is expected the next week the machinery of public affairs in the court is stopped and the attention of all directed to the sweeping of the streets and arranging about his entertainment, and trying to make a good collection of taxes with this pretext.

Traveling in Turkey is constantly interfered with and delayed; the travelers are stopped on their way in many guard stations and are cross-examined, especially if they be Christians; often retained for several days with the excuse of inquiry by telegraph, and sometimes sent back; and are often tied hands and feet and sent to prison, as the fancy of the officer may dictate and the supposed wealth of the accused may suggest.

One exception to this rule of delay must be mentioned—that when the unspeakable Turk unsheathes his "dripping sword" to cut off the heads of "dog giaours" in the name of "Allah the Compassionate and His Apostle" and by command of the all-powerful Padishah—he forgets the words "yavash, yavash;" his thirst for human blood pushes him to extreme activity and madness.

CHAPTER XIX.

THE TURKISH CENSORSHIP.

One of the most ridiculous, injurious and deliberate movements against liberty is the present system and practice of Turkish censorship. It shows the ignorance of the ruling race, the severity of the enslaved officers and the miserable condition of the oppressed people.

1. **The Censor.** An infidel Turk, or, it may be a Christian subject, a wretched slave to the arbitrary will of his ruler, is appointed and forced to examine all the publications and report the result to the higher officer. Such a one must be acquainted with the languages of the country, also with French, and especially with English, which is supposed by the Turk to be the most dangerous means of circulating the seeds of freedom.

We are in a large provincial city, the weekly mail has come, all the books, newspapers and letters for Christians are brought before the Pasha (governor), to be examined before their delivery. The stern Pasha is in his arm-chair smoking his cigarette, several officers are before him to attend his excellent will. The examiner, most probably a Christian young man, is called and seated between the Pasha and the watching officers. The mail-bag is emptied upon the floor, and everything is handed one by one to this young

140

man for examination. His eyes are upon the paper, and all other eyes are upon him closely watching him, not to miss any change of expression on his face. The Pasha says, "What is that paper?" The examiner says, "London Times." "Oh! the cursed paper, we are ordered to withhold it; give it to me." "What is the next?" "Independent." "What does that name mean?" "It means, not subject to the control of others." "Why, that must be a revolutionist paper; let me have it too." "What is this one?" "Science." "Read the contents," "* * * New Discoveries in Bagdad, the capital of the ancient Assyria." "Cut that article and give it to me. What is that other one?" "The Congregationalist." "What?" "The Con-gre-ga-tion-al-ist." "Cursed be that long name; to whom is it directed?" "To Mrs. Cornellia Statenville." "Who is that devil-named man?" "She is a missionary, a hat-wearer." "Curse their hats; what is next?" "An Armenian paper published in Constantinople." "Let me see the seal of the press-official * * * Six copies in one bundle. Oh! crafty hogs! they don't pay their taxes, and sit together and read six papers in one week and learn rebellion against the Highest Wealth (Turkish Government). Put it in the bag and pass to the letters. Be careful now, I had a telegram that giaours are trying to pass arms in air-ships (balloons); there must be something in these letters about that satanic scheme." The letters are examined with greater care, and woe be unto him in whose letter any shadow of suspicion is imagined,

2. **Censorship of Press.** The manuscript of any book must go to the press-officer, who is the president of a committee charged with the sacred duty of ruling over the thoughts, speeches and writings of millions of human beings. The same transactions must be repeated before each edition of the same book. There were so many books officially sanctioned five to fifteen years ago that they are confiscated and prohibited now. This shows that the burden of tyranny is growing heavier. All the books sent from foreign countries must go to the same office, be carefully examined and withheld if some injurious thing is imagined. Any kind of history, geography, even cyclopedias containing articles about Armenia, Turkey, Mohametan religion, etc., are confiscated.

All the unofficial newspapers, Moslem or non-Moslem, must be published in Constantinople, and each proof-sheet of every paper must first go to the censor in order to be examined and corrected, and detained if he deems proper. On every occasion of the Sultan's anniversary, or of the commencement services of the government schools, the papers are expected and even demanded to give full pages in praise of the wisdom and mercy of the Sultan in the official style of the palace slaves. "The late Shah of Persia has died of dropsy." "M. Carnot, of France, has suddenly died of heart disease." Many viziers who have been strangled in the palace were reported in the papers as "died a natural death from sickness to which he was subject a long time, and in spite of all the skill of the doctors could not be saved." These false reports are in all the papers, religious, scientific or political; they are forced to announce these things for their existence, and they do it under the title of "Official News."

The endless reports of these last Armenian massacres which have defiled the whole country from border to border, did not pass beyond being "a small local disturbance in such a place, in which two Moslems and three Armenians were killed, and which was at once suppressed by the soldiers of our gracious Sultan." "Cholera has broken out in such a place, but thanks to the attempts of our gracious Sultan it was immediately controlled and health restored." "A tremendous earthquake occurred in certain places, but thanks to the endless graces and wisdom of our Sultan there was no loss of life but three, and a few wounded." "This year, through the grace of our Sultan, the crops seem to be excellently good." Thus the unfortunate country with all its population and possibilities is flooded by the overflowing stream of "the endless graces" of the Sultan.

3. **Other Illustrations that Touch Directly on Religious Liberty.** From the International Sunday School Lessons of 1893 the title of "Sorrow in the Palace" (Esth. 4:1-9), was suppressed, because there can be no sorrow in *the* Palace, which is called "the region of holy happiness." Also the titles of "Hope in Distress" (Psalms, 38:8-15), "Wicked Devices Frustrated" (Psalms, 33:10-22), and many others, were ordered to be left out. From the religious songs the words "crown," "throne," "fighting,"

"fortress," "soldiers," "victory," "home-land," "trumpet," "kingdom," "enemy," "war," etc., are all stricken out, and all the songs expressing Christian warfare or citizenship or union are canceled. The printing of religious books has been objected to once, on the ground that after having been allowed to have the Bible the Christian subjects have no need of other books. Copies of "Pilgrim's Progress" were confiscated with the idea that they show to the Christian subjects some way to escape from Turkey to a Christian land, from the City of Destruction to Heaven—not an incorrect comparison, however. "The Letters to Families" was stopped with the thought that it might contain something against the government, as it bears the name "letters." A booklet called "The Epistle to the Galatians" was supposed to be a special secret letter to the Christians in Galata (a quarter in Constantinople and a center for Armenians), and the book was stopped. The policemen were sent to the Christian church at Galata to arrest St. Paul, who speaks so deliberately about "the deliverance of this present evil world," and advises his men to "stand fast in the liberty, and be not entangled again with the yoke of bondage." It took much effort and trouble to convince and send these men back, who were more foolish than the ancient Galatians.

The abject ignorance and malice of the censor is best illustrated by the following fact: When he saw in an English book "$H_2 O$," the formula of water (two hydrogen, one oxygen), he supposed it to be a

secret emblem against the Turkish Government, and
after long meditations and consultations he solved it
to mean "Hamid the 2nd (present Sultan) is zero!"
and he insisted that he was correct in his discovery.

The dark shadow of ignorance, the nest of all in-
iquities, is the resting place where "the pearl of
ages" is very anxious to hide himself and his subjects, in spite of the enlightenment of this century.
The Moslem population is the same stupid and lazy
Tartaric race—only they so surpass their fathers in the
addition of hellish horrors upon horrors as to put the
devil in the shade. They show no sign of conscious-
ness of their wretched condition. Some individual
sparks glowing here and there are at once put out
and the national suicide still goes on, and the suffering of the Christian subjects can never be realized.
Under all their bondage, intellectual slavery, blackmailing, poverty and persecution they are groaning
for liberty. But, alas! the world seems totally deaf
to their cries and sighing! It is a mystery of Divine
Providence how the Darkness should be permitted to
rule the Light, and a greater mystery that the most
civilized nations and governments—the supposed
champions of Liberty—would take such a barbarous
nation as the Turks for their friend, and such a
tyrant, the greatest enemy of Christian civilization,
for their ally!

CHAPTFR XX.

1. **Turkish Harem,** which means "the sacred place," is the name given to the ladies' department in the Mohametan home, where no man is allowed to enter without special permission from inside unless he is the husband, father, brother, son, grandfather, grandson, uncle—in short, one of the nearest relatives who could not legally marry the women in the harem. In case of a stranger's inevitable visit each woman over twelve to thirteen years of age must cover her face. The visitor's duty is to stop at the outside of the gate and knock, saying, "Take your veils," and wait for the response from inside. The houses in Turkey are surrounded by a strong thick wall, at least ten to twelve feet high, having only one gateway for entrance, which is kept closed and bolted. Sometimes the husband locks it in the morning and takes the key with him to his business place. Wealthy people have their special department for men entered by a separate gate, and receive their visitors and guests in this department, which is called "Selam lik." A doctor's visit to a harem, which is very seldom among Moslems, is regarded as an exception for the harem law, according to the decree of the Koran that "Necessities modify the prohibition." The ladies of the Imperial Palace were lately vacci-

nated by doctors, stretching out their arms through a hole in the partition between the two departments. The internal management of the harem is sometimes left to colored eunuchs, but commonly the mother-in-law, or in her absence, the chief hanum (lady of the harem) has its charge. Cooking is done in the harem, and the dishes are sent to the men's department through a revolving closet in the partition wall and served by male waiters. The inside of the harem yard must not be seen from any house near or far; hence the law for buildings, especially for windows, is very strict, and the exterior of the houses have the appearance of an ancient castle wall. As the minarets upon which the muezzin crier calls the believers to worship are always higher than the neighboring houses, the women must conceal themselves in the house until the crier makes his brief tour around the minaret. Very often blind men or children are employed in this service, and men of ugly voice are preferred by many pious Moslems, that their wives may not be attracted and tempted to come out of their inner apartments. Some exceedingly fanatic Turks do not allow even the Christian women to enter their harems. Blind men, idiots, eunuchs, and sometimes the old domestic stewards, are allowed in harems.

2. **Polygamy Among the Turks.** Any Moslem who can afford may have four wives in legal marriage, and may have as many concubines as he can purchase or capture. The present Sultan—not the most intemperate of the Ottoman rulers—is said to

have 1,500 women in his harem. By the Mohametan sacred law all the women in the empire belong to
the prophet and his successor on the throne. As
the majority are not able to support many wives they
must be content with a few on this side of the grave,
cherishing the hope that they will have many in the
future paradise. Some rich men, however, prefer to
have only one or two wives, because of the habitual
discord, extravagance and crimes in the larger harems,
where jealousy, slander and constant quarreling are
the daily practice of the "muminehs," the faithful
women.

Marriage is regarded a religious necessity, hence
every man, even the poorest, the maimed and the
crazy, are encouraged to marry, very often the
expenses for wedding being paid by a wealthy aga or
well-to-do neighbors. Their motto is, "A dog can
drag a hide anyhow;" that is, a man can support a
wife anyhow. They also say, "When a person is
created his supplies also are created with him," and
they feel very content with what they may have by
working the least. They marry nearer relatives than
the Christians do. A man must marry his deceased
brother's wife or wives for the sake of preserving
the family inheritance.

3. **The Situation of Turkish Women.** A man
may divorce his wife by simply desiring to do so;
no reasonable cause is demanded of him. A woman
can never demand a divorce, no matter how cruel
and unfaithful her husband may be; she may
be permitted to live separate if she can afford

it. Hence, the only possible way to get rid of a bad husband is to irritate him until he asks for a divorce. There is one point favorable to women— that a husband can not get a divorce unless he first pays the dowry he promised to his wife, according to their wealth and rank, differing from ten to one thousand dollars, or more. The "sheri," the legal branch of the government which attends to marriages and divorces, takes great care on this point to secure and protect the wife's right. A Mohametan may, and often does, marry and divorce the same wife three times by usual transactions of the "sheri" and by the consent of the woman, but not the fourth time unless the woman is married by another man and also divorced by his free will. If a thrice divorced wife is not already married by another man, and if both parties desire a re-union in marriage, the demand of the law is to find another man to marry this woman and divorce her legally, which the poor or the crazy people will do for the sake of money. In some instances, however, the man who was thought crazy proves himself to be so sane as to keep the wife for himself or demands a very large sum for the desired divorce, for which the law does not force him. If a wife be guilty of impurity in matrimony her husband has the right to have her imprisoned by the government for life, or, as the Koran says, "until she finds some divine help to make her escape." The children born of a divorced wife can never be deprived of the right to inherit their father's property, even if they are allowed to live with their mother, in which case the man is forced to pay his children's living until the boy is seven years old and the girl nine.

4. **The Rights of Turkish Women.** Mohamet, being very fond of his mother (who was widowed soon after, or, according to others, just before the birth of the only child) has repeatedly ordered honor and mercy towards mothers, especially widowed mothers. "No man," the Mohametan law says, "can repay the merit of his mother, even if he could carry her on his back all the way to Kabeh," the holy temple in Mecca.

But the same law evidently ranks woman lower than man by limiting, for example, her legal rights. An heiress can only get the half proportion of inheritance that an heir of the same relation may get. The wife can only get one-fifth of the property of her deceased husband if he has bodily heirs from her or from a former wife. A woman can never claim a divorce nor make an objection if her husband marries three wives more and desires to keep concubines. During the husband's lifetime the wife has no claim on his movable or immovable properties, only her dowry and personal ornaments and clothing presented to her. The consequences of the limitation of family rights are mutual hatred, unfaithfulness, crime, and a general degradation of woman. Women are not allowed to attend mosques for the daily prayers; they may have them in the harem. In the month of Ramazan, the fasting month, they are permitted to go to the mosque, but must enter from a special small back door and sit in a gallery enclosed by a thick

lattice work. They can never attend social entertain-
ments unless given by nearest relatives. They are
never allowed to sit at the same table, even with their
fathers, brothers and husbands, if there be a guest
in the house. When they go out of their gates they
must put on a long gown and a thick veil. If they
go with their father, brother or husband, which is
very seldom, they must walk behind. The best part
of the road must always be given to the man. In
the interior of the country if women see a rich man
or an official coming they must sit on the floor and
turn their face to the wall until "His honor" is past.

In villages, these harem ceremonies are not practi-
cable, but the condition of women is far worse.
Their husbands have already purchased them by pay-
ing $10 to $20 in cash, or an ox or a few sheep, or
some pieces of carpets or rugs, or so many bushels of
wheat or barley. Besides the common work of the
house they have their share in all farming work, in
sowing, reaping or pulling the crop with their hands,
carrying it on their backs and threshing it under the
burning sun, which takes weeks, for the lack of
machinery. In such places it is a universal habit
for the man to ride on his horse or donkey, and the
poor woman, often barefooted, walks after him. At
the same time her baby (and perhaps the cradle) is
strapped on her back, or a load of wood or other
burden.

The Turkish women, especially in the villages, are
very free and quick in their talks, having no hin-
drance to use their language. So you can hear

them speaking very clearly and loud, sometimes laughing, sometimes cursing and very often gossiping. When they meet one or more pretty Armenian young people they seldom fail to say, "May plague strike your body," or if they meet a Christian funeral procession, "May Allah cause you all to perish at once," or call loud to the neighbor's wife, "O, Emineh! look this way, a giaour's corpse is going; may all of them have the same destiny by allah," and the other responds, "Amen!" During any uprising against the Christians Turkish women are very happy and always shout and urge the men to slaughter.

5. **The Titles, and Common Sayings about Women.** When you meet with a friend you can never ask about the condition of the women in his house unless you have close relationship with the family; then you must say, "How is the household?" or most intimately, "How is my sister?" or my aunt Emineh?" And he replies, "They kiss your hand." If a man speaks about his wife before others, he never says "My wife" or "Mrs. so and so," but "the people of the house," "your maid-servant," "ash carrier," "sweeper of the house," "the mother of the children," "your sister," etc. A woman is called after her father's name, even if she be married.

Some Turkish proverbs may better show their idea about women: "Woman is a deficient creature." "Woman has long hair, but short mind." "Obey a woman's word but one in forty." "Whip must not

be far from woman." "Do not walk with woman,
else you will suffer calamity." "Woman is the
satan of man." "May allah preserve you from the
evil of woman." "Do not trust the friendship of
woman." "Woman has no religion." "She leaves
confusion among seven quarters." "She loads seven
houses on a donkey and rides also upon it." "You
woman-minded fool!"

They have numerous stories about the evils and
tricks of women. They say, "Satan made a bet
with a woman upon a pair of slippers to see which of
them could cause greater confusion in the world;
and they began the work among the families. After
some time, satan being convinced of woman's
superiority in devices, and fearing that she might one
day harm even himself, he gave up, and putting the
slippers on the end of a long pole, stretched it to the
woman, being afraid to go near her."

6. Turkish Family Discipline. In order to understand the Turkish character, we must go to the foundation, the family discipline. They have no idea and
no word for home. The mother has not her proper
position in the family. Filial, fraternal and paternal
love is not nobler among them than it is among the
pigs—if the comparison is not injustice to the latter.
The jealousy, slander, quarrelling and crimes among
the children of different mothers are terrible beyond
imagination. The defect of the Turkish family discipline does not consist simply of some neglects, but
also positive inducements to corruption. As soon as
the child is able to walk and talk, he is given to the

hands of the meanest of servants (a nurse) to take them where they please, to teach them what they know, to make of them what they may. When they come down from the shoulders of these first teachers they are sent either to schools as corrupt as Sodom, or let loose in the streets to loaf and learn the accumulated corruption of the community, and to harm the Christian children they meet in the streets. If they do not see any giaour to insult and beat, they fight with each other and curse against each other's "faith and religion" and the ancestral graves, etc., most horribly. When several Turks, even the most noted ones, come together and have a little child among them their chief amusement will be, without exception, to make that child utter vulgar words in his broken language. The father of the child, most probably the host of the party, would say to him: "Now, my boy, swear to this uncle's beard," at the same time helping him to speak the necessary words; then says, "Swear to the other uncle's turban," "to that yonder uncle's daughter," "to this young uncle's sweetheart," etc., etc. All will laugh in concert at his each attempt, and praise him for his smartness, and seriously beg long life for him from Allah.

CHAPTER XXI.

1. **A Visit to a Turkish Common School.** The first thing which will attract the visitor's attention is the noise produced in a Turkish school, because every pupil must study his lesson with a loud voice. The exterior appearance of the building, which is generally attached to a mosque, has nothing worthy to be called a school house—a single small room, with very low and narrow windows, if at all. During the cold weather these windows are covered with paper or white thin cotton cloth instead of glass, and in the hot seasons they are left open to the burning sun without any shades, 'unless it be the coats of the students sitting in front of them. There is no chair or desk, or anything like tables. All the children are sitting flat on the floor, on coarse mats or bare boards, which have never seen washing. The teacher is also sitting on the floor, on a small hard cushion, and a little one-foot-high box before him for his table. All the boys (for no girl is allowed in this school) keep small turbaned fezes on their heads, but their shoes or wooden slippers are left at the front door. All the pupils are repeating their lessons in a loud voice, which is stimulated every six or seven minutes by the coarse howling of the long-bearded, large-turbaned and wide, loose-robed man, whom for convenience

155

we shall call Hoja effendi, the lord teacher. These frequent howlings are generally accompanied with a hard stroke of a four-foot-long heavy stick upon the floor its full length, and often with vulgar words.

We can never expect to see anything like maps, black-boards or other school furniture, but only a dirty and badly torn pamphlet in each pupil's hand, in which are some extracts from the Koran in the Arabic language, which the Turkish children do not understand. No geography, arithmetic, natural or unnatural science; and no writing, class system or programme; but beginning from the right hand of the teacher each pupil must come separately and kneel down before him on the bare floor, and after a solemn denunciation of "Satan the Instigator," and recognition of "the name of Allah, the most merciful," must repeat his lesson with a louder voice and chanting tone, all the time swinging the body to and fro. As an approval of the recitation the teacher will simply say "Hum!" two or three times in every line, or sometimes for every single word, even for every syllable if the pupil is spelling. After one or two hundred shut-mouthed "hums!" and an uncertain number of scornful corrections, the so-called lesson comes to its end and the next pupil is called. Of the disapproval or complimentary words that pour out from the mouth of the Haja effendi, the following are comparatively milder ones: "Donkey," "Donkey-headed," "Frozen-brain," "Stiff-skulled," "Lazy donkey," "Blind hog," "Lame dog," "Crippled bear," according to the bodily defects of the children;

"My lamb," "Crazy kid," "Sly fox," "My lion,"
"Black lion," "Black calf," "My son," "My
father," "My brother." In ten minutes he may
call the same boy "Donkey" and "My brother,"
according to the demand of the circumstances.

2. **The Piety of the Hoja Effendi.** Let us not forget to say that our "lord teacher" has also the
charge of the muezzin crier, and the leadership in
public prayer of the mosque. It is about noon; the
children are very tired of sitting and crying their
lessons since the sunrise, also feel very hungry for
food and for mischief. The approach of the "noon-
bread," as they call it, makes them very uncontrol-
lable. The teacher cries with a loud voice and says,
"You hog-pigs! you begin to dig the ground again.
You are almost perished by hunger, Allah may grant
me to see you all perished in one day. No more
patience, impatient dogs! Bring the copper pitcher,
let me have my ablution for noon-prayer, and then
I will send you away; you better had gone to
'jehenem' (hell)! You made my head swell by
causing me to speak so much this morning; may your
heads be swelled like pumpkins and boiled in the
kettle! Bring that pitcher to me." In spite of the
insulting tone of this habitual lecture the pupils run
eagerly to fill the pitcher with cold water and bring
it to the teacher. The teacher cries, "Ah! you
will break it; that is a heritage to me from my grandfather; may Allah have mercy on his soul! Be careful, whosoever breaks that pitcher, by my religion
and faith, I will surely crush his skull. You black-

face Satans, you are in a hurry, not because you love
me, but because you are dying to slip away one
minute earlier; may Allah grant that you may be
paralyzed in your houses and be unable to come here
again. Bring the pitcher this side. * * * 'I seek
refuge by Allah from Satan the accursed' (don't
disturb my mind children, if I rehearse wrong the
sin will be upon your necks), * * * 'in the name of
Allah, the most merciful' (Ahmet, open the doors
of the mosque)." * * * By this solemn ceremony,
mixed with prayer and remarks to the children, the
pious teacher finishes his sacred washing, and turns
again to the children: "Now I will send you to
'noon-bread,' but I have some special notices: first,
do not forget to bring portions to your teacher of
what good dishes you may have at your table; bring
also any kind of fruits, your aunt (teacher's wife) is
not very well, and she will like to have some fruits.
And the next thing I am going to order you is that
you must keep still in your houses and not disturb
your mothers. You see that small bird up that tree?
It always brings me news what mischief you do in
your houses and tells it secretly to my ear. Now I
can tell you all what you did last evening, but for
this time I will forgive you, and watch your conduct
for the next time; you have to come back very soon
and sweep the mosque for to-morrow, which is holy
Friday you know. Look here, I am spitting upon
the ground, and you be sure to be back before it
dries; go now and keep in your mind what I have
said."

3.   A New Pupil Brought to the School.   As the Turkish schools have no vacation, no division of terms and no class system, a new pupil may be brought in at any time.   It is afternoon.   All the children are in their places and a pile of small bundles near the teacher's seat, and he seems quite delighted with them.   A father enters, leading a little boy by the hand, and addresses the teacher: "Peace be unto you, lord teacher."   "And peace unto you, haji aga!   Let us see what is that?"   "What will it be, lord teacher?   I brought your slave to pour water on your hand and to turn your shoes."   "Allah spare his life; you have done very well."   "By Allah, lord teacher, I saw that he was loafing in the streets and I thought if I leave him so he will be a donkey like me."   "Allah forbid, haji aga; may your life be preserved safe from the evils of the devil; you are one of the noblest Muslims of our district.   Oh! the past days; they are gone! What a noble father you had; may Allah illumine his grave.   I can faintly remember your grandfather also; he used to wear, it comes to my mind as a dream, a large green turban, and he always had his long pipe in his hand.   He was a pious Mussulman. Allah may perpetuate his posterity.   By the way, is your mother still living?"   "No, lord teacher, prolonged life for you, she passed five years next winter."   "Is that so?   Oh! Allah may grant long life to you. *** How many children have you?"   "Only this one, your slave, lord teacher?"   "What is his name?"   "Mustafa, lord teacher."   "Oh!

that was my grandfather's name; did you steal his name, little boy? Come here and let me see you." The father leads the child by the hand and taking him nearer to the teacher says, "Now, kneel down and kiss the lord teacher's hand." The teacher says "God bless you, my son." The father continues, "Now, lord teacher, his flesh is yours, his bones are mine; whenever he is disobedient and lazy you may punish him as you please; did you hear it?" Certainly; if he is an obedient boy I will love him just like the light of my eye, but if he is disobedient I will beat him as a dog and imprison him in the dark dungeon under this floor and nail his ear to the wall there and leave him to die with hunger and thirst. I am called crazy Haji, and if once my spirit gets up nobody can control me, even the governor cannot prevent me to do what I decide; I kill men under my feet." "That is all right, lord teacher; he is yours, not mine, do to him as you please. *** What will our debt be to you?" "May your good soul be alive, my dear neighbor; 'parents" and teachers' labors can never be paid enough; may Allah recompense them in the future; still, as a small present for my labors and prayers, I will be content with one cent a week, and five bushels of wheat at harvest time, and several pounds of raisins at fall, and a pair of slippers when your son commences to read the first "juz" (part of the Koran), and a full suit of clothing when he finishes the sacred Koran, by Allah's help." "Very well, sir, all your orders upon my head (I agree), and for the love of Allah, lord teacher, whenever you need something you will let your servant know. I kiss your sacred skirt, lord teacher; take as good care of him as if he was your own son. Good-bye, sir." As soon as he leaves the room the teacher murmurs in a low voice, "You stingy hog, I know what character you are. You promise very easily, but you are not going to fill it. Pay the regular dues and let the extra be a flame to your soul. I knew your cursed father very well; may he not find rest in his grave; he was a man like pieces of nail (useless); are you not the puppy of that dog? But anyhow I have your ears now in my hand. I will make you obliged to pay my wages. Now, boys, to your books; when you see a visitor you leave your work and listen to us like sheep listen to the voice of a flute. Go on! to-morrow is Friday; you have to finish your lessons to-day, else I am not going to send you home to-night. Go on! Read aloud! . . . louder! . . . still louder! . . . that's it."

CHAPTER XXII.

TURKISH HIGHER SCHOOLS.

1. The Essence of Turkish Institutions of Education. Education is not obligatory in the Turkish empire; therefore, the number of the public Turkish schools and the students is considerably smaller compared with other European countries, or even with non-Moslem communities of the empire. During the last twenty to thirty years the government established some public schools in four grades: a primary school for each town, a higher school for each county, an academy for each State and three to four highest institutions in Constantinople for the whole country. The approximate proportion of the numbers of the institutions to that of the population cannot be more than one primary school for 10,000, one higher school for 100,000, one academy for 1,000,000 and one university for the whole population.

The grade of these schools also is very inferior, because with the exception of some Christian professors in the university (?) all the teachers and superintendents are Mohametan fanatics or infidels, unworthy of their position. In the system of instruction there is no radical improvement and can not be as long as the spirit and practice of Islam prevails. That is why the Mohametan students in

European institutions, though very few in number, are generally becoming abject infidels in their hearts and heads, an element which does not seem more favorable to the Christian civilization and a better illustration for the re-entrance of the evil spirit into an empty heart. Hence all the outward appearance of the Turkish education and progress is a total farce, and an extra burden upon the long oppressed and impoverished Christians (for they must contribute to support) and a serious danger for Christian civilization.

2. **A Closer Investigation of These Institutions.** The buildings are better than the common schools, but not as good as one might expect for the large sums collected from the people. The first floor is generally used for the wood and the ashes, and as a place for the shoes, which must not be taken up to the second floor, because it is used for Mohametan worship as well as school. The second floor consists of a narrow hall, to which all the doors of so-called lecture rooms open. No directory, no time-table and no program in the hall, only the emblem (arms) of the Ottoman government. You have to go from door to door and look in to see the contents. One of them looks like an arithmetic class; all the students of the class are crowded before one faded small blackboard and working together in great confusion. The other room looks like a geography or history class. The torn maps are inscribed all over with Arabic letters, reading from right to left. The largest letters on the eastern end read, "The Great

Encircling Sea" (Pacific Ocean). Then comes "Chinumachin" (China); the next attractive inscription reads, "The prosperous countries of the Imperial Ottoman" (Turkey). The Mediterranean is named "White Sea;" Austriah, "The Province of Nemcheh;" Germany, "The Province of Prussia;" France, "The Province of Fransah." When you look more attentively over the map of Turkey you will find that all countries separated from the empire during the last twenty-five to thirty years are put under the same Turkish dominion. Constantinople is called "The Gate of Happiness;" Jerusalem, "The Sacred Holiness;" Damascus, "The Sacred Sham;" Mecca, "The Esteemed Mekkeh of Mysteries;" Medina, "The illuminated Medineh," etc. Both the map and its design carry us back thirty to forty years, and show how the real sciences of geography and history are abused in Turkish schools, which, perhaps, is the reason why an eminent telegraphic officer, a graduate of one of these higher schools, could not be persuaded that "Liverpool" was a single word. He insisted angrily that it was two words—"Liver" and "Pool" —until his Christian subordinate came and ended the dispute. One of the Turkish pashas, the highest provincial officers, hearing from a missionary about the Civil War in the United States, asked him with great surprise: "Why, havaja, did your kings get permission from the Sultan to declare war against each other?" During the last Russo-Turkish war the copies of a telegram were pasted on the walls, telling that "near Alashehir the Moscows suffered such a defeat before the Ottoman braves that the blood of the enemy formed a river so deep as to reach the breasts of the horses of the Ottoman cavalry." And the large-turbaned Turks, who thought the telegraph to be a devil's operation, were heard by this time reporting that this news was produced by itself all over the country, while the secret dispatch was passing from Constantinople to Mecca.

3. **Commencement Services in Turkish High Schools.** It is the "Prize day," as they call it. In one of the largest halls of the town, teachers, students and their friends, and many invited persons, are crowded; the service is not yet begun, though the announced time has already passed one hour; the air in the room is almost unbearable; a great many are smoking, walking out and in, talking with a tremendous confusion and noise. Some are going out to drink and bringing a pail of water in for their friends, others calling for "a drop of that water," some trying to reach the pail, laughing, cursing—everything but order. Later on, the pasha, the chairman of the service, comes in, followed by a dozen well-armed soldiers and about all the officers and influential men of the town (there can be no woman in this assembly). By this time the whole congregation rises, as an homage to the pasha and his followers, and a military band begins to play the "Hamidieh March," at the close of which, all being seated, the chairman comes forward, and taking a paper out of his pocket begins to read it as the

opening address of the exercises. The subject of
that paper is praise for the Sultan; the style is
oriental, poetic and adorned; the language as high
as possible, full of Persian and Arabic words and
phrases, and the tone of reading low, monotonous
and quivering.

In order to make our readers better acquainted with
the contents of said paper, we shall attempt to trans-
late some parts of it, according to the capacity of the
English language in expressing oriental formality:
"By the boundless grace and endless mercy of the
Lord of all creatures on earth and in heaven, and
under the safest shadow of the world-stretched wing
of his Imperial Majesty, our Sovereign and Sultan,
the king of all kings and the crown-giver of all the
princes of the world, we, the most humble subjects
of the glorious Ottoman empire and sons of the
sacred and most prosperous countries, are privileged
to assemble here to-day to perform our usual sacred
duty in sincerely praying for the utmost prosperity
and longevity of our powerful, gracious and great
padishah, and for the constant welfare of his highest
commonwealth. Since the happiest day of the
glorious enthronement of his Imperial Majesty, the
greatest, wisest of all the rulers of the universe, we
most fortunate subjects of the pearly throne—the
glory of which equals the brightness of the celestial
constellations—have always been enjoying innu-
merable and marvellous signs of his bottomless
ocean of wisdom and unparalleled prudence, which is
the miraculous heavenly gift to the worthiest of all

the monarchs upon thrones. By this delightful chance we acknowledge once more our most pleasant privilege to offer the emblems of our true faithfulness and complete obedience to the heaven-like threshold of his imperial glory, the conqueror, the most gracious and the powerful majesty, our merciful father, Sultan Hamid, the Great, by repeating 'Long live my Padishah!' Amen! and Amen!!''

4. **The Relation of Christian Subjects to Their Schools.** The Turkish high schools are nominally for all the subjects of the empire, but there are very few Greeks and Armenians who could find any way to enter them. Especially during these last fifteen years the non-Moslem element is remarkably enfeebled in these institutions. Still the expenses are paid by all communities of the country. The Christians invariably prefer to have their own high schools and colleges for their young men and women, and for further advancement appeal to the European or American institutions. When a doctor or lawyer from foreign schools desires to practice in Turkey he has to go to Constantinople, spend his money and time and be examined before the Turkish faculties, to procure his certificate or their permission. The native Christian students are subjected to very severe examination and restriction.

CHAPTER XXIII.

TURKISH LIFE AND CUSTOMS.

1. **The Scenery in a Turkish Street.** The Turkish cities are generally in good locations. The streets are narrow, irregular and dirty. The houses are large and strong, but not attractive. They have but few and small windows, and are on the second floor. Every house is surrounded by a high and thick stone wall, with only one gateway, which is locked or barred day and night. In the interior of Turkish houses, from the most destitute to the most elegant and royal, in the houses of poverty and wealth, we find the same degree of sin and misery.

The scenes and events of a Turkish street cannot be told on paper. Muleteers and carriage men drive and curse their animals and cry to the passing multitude, "Be careful; let it not touch you." Street sellers are crying in every style and tone. Porters are carrying heavy burdens on their backs. Dervishes are howling and the fortune-tellers prophesying. The public criers are making official announcements: "O, Moslem servants! may Allah give long life to our padishah (Sultan)! Hereafter whoever walks in the streets after three o'clock in the evening (three hours after sunset), whether he has a lamp or not, will be arrested and imprisoned and heavily fined; this is the command of his excellency, our governor.

168

Hear! you will have no excuse hereafter." Another: "Since last night a donkey is lost. Its tail is short; one front leg is lame; its hair is gray. Whosoever saw it will have three piasters, and whosoever finds it will have - five piasters. Come! and make the owner glad."

In.this Babylonian confusion many children, large and small, curse and cry. The pasha (governor) passes from his harem to his office with half-a-dozen servants before him and a dozen officers behind him. Everybody must recognize him by stopping and bowing, almost touching the ground with the back of the right hand, then lifting it up to their lips and then to their forehead in perfect silence. He returns this homage by a slight motion of his right hand. The countless hungry dogs are barking and biting each other, and sometimes trying to attack the passers-by, in imitation of their legal protectors (Moslems).

2. **Traveling in Turkey.** The Arabic proverb, "Traveling is a portion of hell," is applicable to Turkey, for there is no facility, no safety, and therefore no pleasure, even in a country which is unique for its natural beauty and healthy climate; no bridges over the large rivers, no prepared roads in miry places, no wide passages on the precipices. The only means of transportation are large camels, lazy horses, small donkeys and mules, and sometimes oxen and cows, driven by muleteers—the very ignorant villagers. In all Asiatic Turkey there is not more than 400 miles of railroad, therefore all journeys must be made by animals or walking, with an average of

twenty miles a day. The animals are meanly fed in summer on grass, in winter on straw and very little barley. On winter nights the animals and the riders are sheltered together under the same roof of a khan (a rude, low and large building with only one room). There can be no fixed plan for the day. If you ask the muleteer the distance to the next town, khan or stream, he answers, "O, it is just here; about half an hour." You go on for hours and ask again, and get the same answer. You ask, "Where will you spend the night?" He replies, "Allah knows; I don't know; wherever the night comes we will halt there; don't worry about it; these places are very dangerous; the other day highwaymen killed three merchants and captured all their properties just in yonder valley."

In traveling, women, and especially children, are carried in mafa (two boxes), fastened one on each side of the horse. Owing to the constant dangers the travelers have to go in caravans (a large company of muleteers and passengers, with scores of various animals). They have carriages in the sea coast cities and in some parts of Anatolia, but for the lack of safety and regularity they are not of much use.

3. **Language and Conversation of the Turks.** The Turkish language, being composed of coarse Tartaric dialect and Persian and Arabic words and phrases, has its own beauty when spoken by the educated, but among the uneducated it represents the coarsest mode of speech. Turkish conversation is characterized by many and unnecessary adjectives,

exaggerations and obscenity, spoken in an imaginative and proverbial style. Among the educated the rule is that the first person of the pronoun is expressed in humblest style and the second person just the contrary, for instance: I—"your servant," "your humble servant," "your most worthless slave;" you— "your highness," "your excellency," "your highest excellency;" how are you—"how is the honored pleasure of your excellent nobility?" The answer is, "your servant kisses the sacred hands of your highest personality."

The Turkish style of addressing a letter: "By the grace of the Most High. Behold this letter is offered to the sacred direction of sagacious Ali Effendi, the assistant clerk in the financial department of the County of Keller, in the State of Bagdad."

In anger and quarreling the following expressions are very commonly used: "May your eyes be blinded, and you be left by the walls helpless;" "may your bread run from you on horseback, and you pursue it on foot and never reach it;" "may you not own two garments;" "may your lamp be extinguished suddenly" (die); "may you fall down like a pine tree;" "may melted lead be poured into your ears;" "may you be a vagabond in your life, and be dead in a stormy day;" and many indecent words which we can not put here.

The expressions for good wishes also are many and flattering, as: "May God hold your hands;" "may God build your household;" "whatever you touch as dust may be turned to gold;" "may Allah give you a dark-eyed sweetheart;" "may you enjoy the benefit of your child;" "may your enemies be blinded," etc.

4. **Some Turkish Riddles, Proverbs and Love Songs.** "When I go it goes galloping behind me." (Shadow.)

"A well and water in it, and a snake in the water with a pearl in its mouth." (A lamp.)

"It can jump down the mountain without hurt, still it cannot step in a stream." (Paper.)

"If you tie, it goes; if you let it loose, it stops." (Shoes.)

"It is woman that builds or ruins a house."

"The girl makes a woman like her mother."

"He begs at the door of St. Sophia, and gives alms at Sultan Ahmed." (Two mosques that are very near each other in Constantinople.)

"When you ask a lazy man to work he will preach you a long sermon."

"Two captains sink the ship."

"Little bread, peaceful head." (Content and peace.)

"Death is a black camel that kneels before every door."

"He tries (in vain) to dig a well with a needle."

"A stone rolled into the well by a fool, cannot be taken out by forty wise men."

"Know the man by his friends."

"He who eats without desire digs his grave with his teeth."

"He thinks he has created the small mountains." (Shows vanity.)

"Eh, no money, no money,
In his pocket no money;
Unminding his blindness,
That fool man tries to own me."

"I'll tell you don't madden me,
Or I'll cut your willow-tree;
If you marry some one else,
I'll surely leave this country."

"Water pail in hand has she,
Walks to the fount slowly;
Girl, your sweetheart is coming,
Run back homeward, make hurry."

"Moon rises leaping, leaping,
Through the branches peeping;
I have got sad news to-day,
My love for me is weeping "

"My daughter, pearly, pearly,
Soon grow be a lady;
I ll marry you a gypsy,
Play your gong, be happy."

5. Miscellaneous Customs Among the Turkish People.—*Medication.* They do not use many medicines, and those which are used are such things as the blood of a black hen, the skin of a black cat, certain animals' manure, roasted snake, the mixture of seven flowers from seven fields, the milk of a woman who nurses a girl baby, the fat of the bear, the milk of a bird, the rain-water that falls in the month of April, and other things that cannot be found easily, if at all. They believe in supernatural power of relics, reading from Koran, touch of a dervish, favorable words of an idiot, the tombs of certain saints, waters of certain fountains, threads bound around the wrist by a witch, or rags tied to certain bushes.

Eating. They sit flat upon the ground and eat from the same dish with wooden spoons, or dip the bread, which, being thin and soft, is folded like a dipper or cup-shape. As a rule, women do not eat with men; they have their black coffee after each meal. Tea is very little used among the Turks; wine never, but brandy and other liquors are much used. Among the fruits, grapes are used the most, because they are plenty and very cheap. They are gluttonous in their eating; their motto is, "never mind the death of a horse if it is from barley."

Dreaming. They give vital importance to dreams. To dream of a white horse is wealth, riding upon it is gaining wealth; of red color is some event which is going to take place soon; of a girl is some "hot news;" of fifth, is luck; of a Christian priest, is angel; of water is trouble, bathing is bad. Pulling the tooth in a dream shows the death of some friend, the nearer to the back teeth the worse. To take food from the hand of a dead friend is an ill-omen for the taker.

Burial. They bury their dead as soon as possible, while the sun is up. The corpse is washed with hot water and soap and wrapped in a white, cotton cloth like a mummy. The body is put in a long bier (frame) and carried upon the shoulders of four men, changing hands frequently for an honor to the dead, and for the religious merit which is promised by Mohamet to those who carry a Moslem corpse seven steps. A religious service is held in the cemetery by all the friends and neighbors, which is a common

Mohametan prayer. They believe that the departed soul unites with them in that prayer. At the end of the prayer the priest asks the opinion of the congregation about the character of the deceased. If two among them can give favorable testimony the soul goes to happiness.

6. **A Common Turk's Idea about the Foreigners.** As the Turks never wear hats and do not allow their Christian subjects to have them (except in a few seacoast cities), the common name given to the foreigners is "hat-wearers," and when they are angry at them they use indecent expressions for their hats, blue eyes and whiskers. When the American travelers happen to pass through a Turkish village and stop at the edge of the town, the people come and gather around them, looking amazed; and if some lady is found in the company the women come near by and touch her hat, clothing and jewelry, and ask about their prices. They will not forget to ask whether she is married or not; if they get a negative answer, they seem surprised, and inquire the reason. If they get a positive answer, they ask which one of the gentlemen is her husband; has she children and how many, and why she did not bring them with her, etc.

Ninety-nine in a hundred Turks have never heard the name of America, and nine in ten who have heard have not the right idea what and where "Amelikan" is. All foreigners are called "Frank." Russia, their immediate neighbor and memorable enemy for centuries, is called "Mosgof" (Moscow), and her people

"Black giaour," "Blind Mosgof," "Blind hog."
They say "Hog Frank has sharp mind." They call
a railroad (without having seen it), "ship on the
land;" bicycle, "the devil's horse." Balloon is called
"ship in the air," and they talk about Armenians
having passed arms and ammunition into the interior
through these "air-ships," and even some have
declared that they saw them passing in the night.
They say "Frank can destroy a whole army by holding a huge looking-glass against the sun and burning
the enemy with its light," and sometimes use this
means by night. They think about the telegraph that
you strike here and the words are heard at the other
end. They are very cautious not to touch the wire,
thinking that it will cause wrong news at the other
end, and you will be held responsible for it. When
they hear the sound produced upon the wires by the
wind they say, "There, the news is going!"

Some think that "the people in the interior'"
(Europe) walk with their heads down, and there are
people in China that have one eye, which is at the
top of their heads. When they hear an American
talk English they say "he is talking bird language,"
and ask the native Christians whether they know this
language. If they say "no," they are surprised and
ask "Why do they not talk giaourish" (infidelist)?
All the customs of the foreigners seem to them very
strange and unnatural, especially their tables, where
men and women sit together, talk and laugh while
eating. They most bitterly detest the foreigners, be
they missionaries or merchants, for their neglect to

invite the stranger or visitors to eat who may happen to come in while they eat, because hospitality is the highest ideal of every Oriental.

CHAPTER XXIV.

THE CAUSES THAT LED TO THE ARMENIAN MASSACRES.

Two of the fundamental causes which underlie every Turkish massacre have already been discussed in the previous chapters. namely: The anti-Christian spirit of Islam and the savage nature of Tartaric blood. Besides these general causes, there were some special motives which led "The Gracious Father of the Ottoman Empire" to these late deeds of unparalleled devastation and death.

1. **The Multiplication of the Armenians in the Empire Excited the Jealousy of the Turks.** The last and careful census made about twelve years ago perplexed the Turkish Government over the unexpected and sad condition of numbers of the people. Armenians, as Christian and civilized people, live a moral life, regarding also the physical and hygienic laws; on the other hand, the Turks were not only slow in increase, but were found diminished in numbers. This decrease was due to several reasons, such as the practice of polygamy, vice of abortion, constant supply of military troops and loss of life in wars, ignorance and carelessness in respect to the laws of health, and fatalistic refusal of preventive and curative means in times of epidemics, which are frequent in Turkey. Besides, a goodly portion of the country was severed from the empire since the last Russo-

178

Turkish war, which caused considerable decrease in the number of the Mohametan element. All these things were facts which the Armenians could not help, and the Turks would not stand indifferent. It was repugnant and alarming to the haughty Mohametan to see the multitudes of Christians in the streets on Sundays and young "infidels" crowding the roads on their way to and from schools every day.

According to the last "Scheme of the Armenian Reforms," prepared by the representatives of the six great Powers and forcibly signed by the Sultan, the governors in the six provinces should be elected in proportion with the numbers of two parties. This would create a great change in the fabric of the old despotism, securing some Armenian governors to the first position. Hence the question of numbers was the crisis of "To be or not to be" in the palace and the porte.

2. **Turks were Jealous of the Increasing Wealth of the Armenians.** As a reaction of the Armenian dark ages, which continued from the middle of the fourteenth to the middle of the nineteenth century, these last forty to fifty years offered a better chance for commercial movements, especially to those who live in large towns and seaports where there was more safety and freedom. The long suppressed business ability of the Armenian race showed itself in the banks and commercial circles of the capital and provincial centers; extending its branches also in every commercial city of Europe and of the United States. Even the greatest distance of the British

colonies could not prevent them from the search and accumulation of wealth. They transported the silky wool and superior hides of Armenia to the markets of Egypt, and brought the costly indigo blue to the doors of Armenian dyers. They put the delicious pistacio nuts in the French confectioneries, and exchanged the money for delicate European dry goods; hunted all the old rugs from the oriental parlors and furnished the halls of the United States with them. The Armenians of the Harpoot district, mostly common laborers in the New England factories, were known to send to their friends $5,000 weekly to purchase acres of land from their Turkish and Kurdish neighbors.

There was a commercial revival among the Armenians. The young men, more vigorous than their conservative fathers, took out the buried treasures and began a strong competition with the Moslems, and succeeded. The big-turbaned Turk and the ragged Kurd, together with the barefooted Arab, began to ask the way to the Armenian banks to borrow money for their antediluvian plowing work, at the same time sighing in their souls and murmuring in each other's ears, "I wish I had the giaour's mind and wealth."

The young Armenian minds, enlightened with "the modern civilization," began to think that the gunpowder stores of the Turk were emptied, and that the sharp teeth of Tartaric brutality had becomes dull, and especially that the originators and protectors of the modern civilization would never allow the repetition of the old barbarities against the honor of humanity and glory of Christianity. Relying on these realities, which soon proved to be mere dreams of delirious minds, they dared to show their heads out of the dark cellars of their ancestors, and began to build good houses and live as honorable men among degenerate semi-barbarians.

3. **The Progressive Schools of the Armenians Made the Turks very Jealous.** In one of the previons chapters the reader had a description of the Turkish schools. The late changes are not radical, and cannot be under the circumstances. Now we are in an Armenian school; it is the examination day; the governor of the city, with all his turbaned and military companions, is invited (as should be done), and held the best seats in the clean and quiet hall. The teacher calls a boy, not more than twelve years old, and asks him how many hours are in a week. He answers at once, 168. The teacher asks again, how many minutes are in a week; the child finishes the problem quickly, and says 10,080. The governor looks around at his subordinates and expresses his wonder for the smartness of that "one inch tall" boy. The teacher gives a third question: "How many seconds are in a year?" The governor calls aloud to the cadi (Turkish judge), asking whether he could find that out; he says, "Not indeed, by prophet." He asks the chief clerk of the court, and he answers, "No, sir, by Allah." The governor says to the judge and the clerk: "If I order a donkey's head cooked, can you eat it all?" Before the clerk

gives his answer to this complimentary question our boy reads his figures on the board with a clear voice and pronunciation. The Turkish officers are ashamed of themselves; but this feeling does not produce in them a true competition, but a jealous spirit to retard the one who is making progress.

Science and education are always held in great esteem by every Armenian, but there never was a time in their history more noted for rapid and brilliant progress than these last thirty or forty years. Almost in every town numerous and graded schools were established and managed by competent principals, mostly educated in European or American schools. Armenian literature has got a new life, and journalism, even in its narrow space, made remarkable progress. Several daily papers were full of articles about the living questions of Christian civilization and progress. French has become almost common in the schools. English is highly cultivated, especially in the Protestant institutions, which are not few in number or inferior in grade. The Russian, German and Italian languages have had their entrance among the Armenians, who have a proverbial name of being linguists.

Armenians gave also a remarkable impulse to Turkish literature. Muhendisian made the best and most varied types of Turkish letters, and saved the reader from the unendurable troubles of the old style cryptograms. Arakel, Caspar and other publishers contributed marvelously to the production and circulation of Turkish books. Some eminent teachers, as Apikian and Bogos, prepared the best grammars and dictionaries of the Turkish language. This, too, made the Turks jealous that giaours were better acquainted with their business and books than themselves. In an old style Turkish school the Arabic grammar was a life work, while in the Armenian schools the necessary principles of that language are simply a few months' work. Many poor and honest Armenian young men gain name and position through education, while hosts of Turkish boys are loafing in the streets and stepping over wild street dogs and building a character worse than dogs.

4. **Armenians, Noble Aspiration for Christian Liberty Excited the Wicked Turk.** In spite of continuous and severe p rsecutions of ages the fire of freedom was never quenched in the soul of the Armenian. The exiled young professor's last sighs from the depths of Siberian gloom have always and everywhere found their echo in the hearts of his countrymen: "I will be true to thee till death; yea, even upon the gallows' tree the last breath of a death of shame shall shout thy name, O Liberty!" Their contact with the civilized part of the world and their enlightenment by the dawn of Christian education added much upon this *natural* and holy aspiration. Aided by the American and English Bible Societies, they translated the Holy Scriptures and some other books into the Turkish language, and in some parts of the empire they evangelized and baptized the dialect of the oppressor, with the long-cherished aspiration of evangelizing them, too. When the British

Ambassador said, "Soon the Christians will be able to preach the gospel in Mohametan pulpits," there was a general shouting of jubilee, not that the Armenians would have a chance to slaughter Turks in their mosques, but that they would have the freedom and privilege of bringing their neighbors to the knowledge of true salvation. They did not take any aggressive course against the Turks or other Moslem communities, but rather, taking the favorable proclamations of the Sultan as sincere, cherished the expectation that both parties, hand in hand, would try to elevate the country to the level of European prosperity.

While the Armenians were thus hopeful and aspiring, the fanatic Turk kept swinging his head and sighing, "Alas! Islam lost its power and glory; the field remained in the hands of giaours!" The deep-rooted enmity that drew this exclamation out of the bigoted Turk was not idle, but by a gradual advance prepared and accomplished horrors too terrible to describe and too deep to realize.

CHAPTER XXV.

Confronted by the facts mentioned in the preceding chapter, the Turk could not stand indifferent. He had two alternatives, to submit or to oppose. He could appreciate the vitality of this progressive element in his dominion, and, laying aside every prejudice and fanaticism, endeavor to rebuild his decayed government, or take his ancient policy of reducing the Christians low by plundering their accumulated wealth and crushing their honor and aspirations under his feet. He preferred the latter policy, and by Satanic devices prepared the way of destruction in the following steps:

1. **The First Step Was to Have a Fanatic and Narrow-Minded Sultan.** In 1876 Sultan Aziz was dethroned and secretly murdered with the apparent accusation of "Abusing the Treasury (!) of the Highest Commonwealth." Just three months later his nephew and successor, Sultan Murad, was deposed with the accusation of "Sick-mindedness." Perhaps both accusations were true; yet who can say that nine in ten Sultans did not abuse the wealth of the government and have a sound and practical mind? The fanatic and adventurous party of the palace was after another thing; they planned to have a Sultan that

185   -

could be used as an instrument in their hands. Prince
Hamid, the brother of Sultan Murad, was the man.
Exceedingly timid and suspicious in nature, feeble in
structure, short-sighted in mind, devoid of education,
and especially fanatical in religion, Prince Hamid,
who was every moment fearing the assassinator's approach, was put on the throne and given the
titles of "The Finest Pearl of the Age," "The Esteemed Center of the Universe," "The Sultan of the
Two Shores and the High King of the Two Seas,"
"The Crown of Ages and the Pride of All Centuries," "The Greatest of all Caliphs," "The Shadow
of God on Earth," "The Crown-giver of all the
Princes of the World," "The Gracious Father,"
"The Victorious Sultan Abdul Hamid Khan," etc.

Among the palace party there were men clever
enough and able to make plans for the diabolical
steps to be taken in the future. Some proselyte
Christians, some European adventurers, had the light
and mind to study the inner and the outer condition
of the country and prepare reports for the mechanical endorsement of the Sultan. By the strict police
system of the palace and suspicious guardianship of
the imperial harem, it was impossible to see the oper-
ations which were going on in that "region of holy
happiness," as it is called. All the telegraphic and
postal transactions were in the hands of the palace
favorites; they could modify, annul or invent any
news they thought favorable for their policy. The
Sultan was but a slave in their hands.

Gradually "the seat of the prophet" (palace) became the center and the den of the most cruel butcheries and unheard of tortures. Any Ottoman subject, be he a Turk or Christian, a common student or vizier, a stranger or relative to the palace, upon the slightest suspicion or false accusation unfavorable to their plans, would be summoned to the horrible circles of "the star palace" and put to death. The bottom of the Bosphorus and Marmoral waters were covered with the bones of slaughtered students and officers, men and women of the imperial harem, until all the authority remained in the hands of a degenerate Arab slave called Aziz Effendi, who blotted the history of the nineteenth century with infamous deeds of cruelty and vice.

2. **The Second Step** was to caress and enthuse the fanaticism of the Moslem population and show them that a zealous and true caliph was occupying the sacred seat of the prophet. It was very easy to deceive the ignorant. Sultan Hamid ordered several mosques and tekkiehs to be erected around the palace and bigoted shiekhs were rallied in them and encouraged to practice their religious services under the supervision of "the pious sovereign," who himself was very regular to attend these mosques for his Friday noon prayer, which is called "selamlik" (the procession of the Sultan and the princes and all civil, military and religious chief officers, encircled by thousands of soldiers and spectators).

The public criers repeatedly walked in the streets and bazaars of Constantinople to inform the Moslem population of the absolute will of the Sultan that the women cover their faces with veils when they went in the streets—which met the ideal of the fanatic majority—and the necessity of Ramazan fasting was discussed and enforced everywhere. The ruined mesjids and the Mohametan chapels were repaired and opened for public prayers and the believers were enforced to attend them. The schools were started and religious leaders were sent to neglected Moslem villages and towns. Lightning-stricken minarets were repaired and the unceasing cry of muezzin was heard upon them. The disputed properties of the mosques were secured from the hands of the local beys or agas and delivered into the hands of the clergy. The annual pilgrim caravan of the Sultan, loaded with great riches and in Oriental pomp, started on its journey in the streets of Scutari, and continued for weeks, until the heavy-laden camels sat in front of the door of the kabeh, the holy temple at Mecca. The sacred mantle of the Prophet Mohamet, kept in the closets of the old seraglio, was kissed by the Sultan and all palace authorities every 14th of Ramazan, the memorial day of Mohamet's "journey to Heaven." The holy banner of the religious wars, ever ready to lead the Moslem hosts against the "infidels," showed itself in the hand of "the conqueror," Sultan Hamid—though he has never been out of the capital since his enthronement.

This central zeal made its favorable effect felt in the remotest parts of the empire, and a very great majority of the Moslem population thought Sultan

Hamid II. as one of the most proper representatives in the chair of Mohamet.   And the spirit of Islam took a new fire all over the country, and the chronic anti-Christian enthusiasm began to boil the blood of the followers of Islam.

3.. **The Third and a Natural Step** was the restraint put on the Christian subjects.   This began to show itself in the slow and gradual exclusion of the Armenian students and officers from their positions. Then the number of Armenian schools and churches was decreased by not allowing the new ones to be established, and closing some of the former ones for trifling reasons.   Sultan Hamid is said to have given firmans only for one new Armenian church near the frontiers of Russia, and for the repairing of a few, while he ordered scores of churches and schools and other institutions to be disbanded.   Almost all literary, educational, charitable and economical societies, even the Young Men's Christian Associations, were prohibited and dissolved when discovered.   The programs of the schools and the text-books were minutely examined.   Armenian and universal histories, geography and readers, which contained direct or indirect allusions to the above subjects, foreign atlases, statistics, historical novels, all were confiscated and officially prohibited.   Teachers who could not be made blind instruments in their hands were expelled, imprisoned, tortured, and in many cases killed.   Christian doctors, lawyers, merchants and influential members were arrested by false accusations. Even the priests and the ministers of the gospel were not left out of this detrimental persecution.

Correspondence and traveling were strictly guarded and almost entirely prohibited. Immigration to any foreign country, and even to the Turkish seacoast cities was absolutely forbidden to the Armenians. Many Armenians who had official pass-ports for some Turkish city, as Constantinople, Smyrna or Beirout were arrested, imprisoned in the ports of Trebizond, Samsoun, Mersina and Alexandretta or sent back to their own town. All the Armenians who escaped to Europe or the United States could do so only by suffering terrible hardships and perils and by bribing the police. An Armenian was several times captured and sent back to Harpoot, and at last, in his sixth attempt, succeeded in reaching a French steamer for the United States by swimming about two miles to where it was anchored.

The clergy and influential men were forced to sign false reports or accusations prepared by the government. Blackmailing became a universal practice among the Turkish officers, every town and village was besieged, every road was watched by detectives and officious officers ever ready to rob the innocent. The news of the Sassoun massacres in 1894 was not heard in other parts of Armenia and Asia Minor until four months after the event. No one could go safely in the streets with a manuscript in his pocket, however harmless it might be. Any policeman would at any time attack him and get the paper and take it, with its owner, before the governor, who, generally without examination, would order the poor Armenian to be imprisoned. Several days, and very often weeks, would pass until that paper—perhaps a mother's letter or a discourse on botany—could be handed to its owner and several hundred piasters demanded for his release. *If* that paper had contained anything directly or indirectly about the government, or some words that the examiner's arbitrary and vicious will could give an unfavorable interpretation, the poor man could not expect to come out of his prison.

Turkish Prisons are always attached to the city hall and in its dark and damp basement. These prisons, far from being the means of correction, are the most terrible device of bribery, vengeance, cruelty and suffering, especially for the poor Christians who are shut in these subterranean hells under the name of political prisoners. For them there is no law, no justice, no conscience and no name. Exposed to cold, hunger, thirst, flogging, bodily tortures of every description, made to squat in deep mud, sitting in freezing water, pulling out of mustache and beard, hanging head downward, burning portions of the body with red-hot tongs, pouring filth over the head, burying the head in manure and violation of personal honor, these are the common tortures which could be mentioned among the various unspeakable brutalities perpetrated upon the poor, helpless Christians daily.

"The Inquisitorial dungeons of the Middle Ages," says one, "may be regarded as paradise compared with these nineteenth century hells of Turkish barbarity."

4. Another step as a preparation for the Armenian massacres was the organization of the "Hamidieh troops." These troops, which consisted largely of Kurdish chiefs and their allies, were at first supposed to be the means of precaution against the impending invasion of Russian Kossacks from Caucasia, near Kurdistan, but soon after it was clearly seen that the plan was for an internal massacre of the Armenians, with whom these Kurdish tribes lived for centuries, sometimes on friendly terms and very often in severe enmity. The Turks, however fanatical they may be, are cowardly and lazy, especially prone to plunder property and outrage women, while Kurds, not inferior in the same barbarities, are ferocious murderers. During the last massacres how often the leaders of the government were heard to cry aloud among the mobs, "Stupid Turks! you are absorbed again in plunder and are not killing giaours! Kill the men, and the women, and the property will naturally be yours! Kill the bee, and the honey is yours! Allah!" And this is a proved fact, that wherever the Kurdish Hamidieh troops were let loose, as in Ourfa, Gurin, Severek, Egin, etc., the devastation and butchery was complete. Kurds are more murderous than religious Moslems, and whenever the drum of slaughter sounds in their ears they can not control their bloodthirsty natures, be it excited against Christians or Turks. In the history of Turkish militia this organization may be regarded the most malicious device next to that of Janissaries.

CHAPTER XXVI.

SO-CALLED ARMENIAN REVOLUTIONISTS.

1. Armenia's Appeal to Europe Considered Rebellion. As the natural result of Christian civilization, the Armenians could not help cherishing in their hearts the sacred ambition of freedom, as a living plant could not help bursting into life under the necessary conditions of nature. Being oppressed and deprived of this human privilege, they could not help sighing under the heavy burden of Turkish persecutions and Kurdish outrages. Who can blame them for feeling such pain and pleading for any help that might be offered?

The presentation of their deplorable condition before the representatives of the Great Powers, as they did in the Berlin Conference in 1878, was simply to implore their help in suppressing the Kurdish and Circassian cruelties, and obliging the porte to regard the promises of reform, which were entirely cast into oblivion, especially after learning that the European governments had repeatedly shown themselves anxious in securing these promises of the Sultans and pretending zealousness for their fulfilment.

A pamphlet lately published under the title of "England's Responsibility Towards Armenia," by Canon McCall of the Anglican Church, contains evidence enough to prove from the Blue Books of the

British government for the past *fifty* years that the condition of the Armenians was as deplorable as ever under the tyranny of Turks and Kurds, and the indifference of the English government to suppress these atrocities, which it was her duty to do, according to her treaties and promises. The terrible reports mentioned in these Blue Books were all written by the British consular agents residing in Armenia, and contain all the details of events. The Armenians, being unaware of this indifference on the part of the English government, have made repeated appeals to Christian England, and through her to Europe, for succor.

Especially, knowing that in this century Greece, Roumania, Bosnia, Montenegro, Servia and Bulgaria were liberated from the tyrant of ages, and Lebanon, Samos, Crete and Egypt had gained especial privileges, all through the aid of European powers, Armenia would and might naturally desire and implore of the same Powers for a reformed and just administration under their guarantee. Moreover, the Czar Nicholas of Russia has promised the Armenian nation to furnish her with some kind of provincial government under the care of the Russian throne.

The sixty-first article of the Berlin Treaty, signed by the six great Powers of Europe, reads as follows: "The Sublime Porte undertakes to carry out, without further delay, the improvements and reforms demanded by local requirements in the provinces inhabited by the Armenians, and to guarantee their security against the Circassians and Kurds. It will periodically make known the steps taken to this effect to the Powers, who will superintend their application.'' Can the Armenians be blamed for their anticipation of interference by the Powers, who pledged themselves for their protection?

2. **Hunchag, the Supposed Armenian Conspirator.** The atrocities which were promised to cease after the solemn Berlin Treaty) have continued and increased systematically and in such rapidity, and committed even before the eyes of the Signing Powers for seventeen long and weary years, that the Armenians have lost all hopes of any assistance from abroad. In Armenia proper the Kurdish and Turkish tax-gatherers succeed each other and plunder what is left, and commit such atrocities that cannot be told in a public book like this. At last the helpless Armenians said to the Turkish officers: ''The Kurds left nothing to pay you; here we are, take what you find; we do not know who is our ruler, the Turk or the Kurd. If you are our masters, protect us against these Kurds.'' This pleading and just protest was taken as an open declaration of rebellion and soon was telegraphed to the palace of the Sultan, who was already watching for this opportunity to commence his infernal plan. A few young teachers and students who took their education in Germany and Russia, and had some socialistic air in their religious creed, taught the people to bring the above-mentioned protest before the Turkish tax-gatherers under the said condition of affairs. These few hot-headed young men and their very few

co-thinkers, who called themselves "Hunchag" (sounding instrument), and were ranked by some empty-minded or malicious writers with Anarchists and Nihilists, could have been easily arrested and controlled if the Turkish government had any intention of doing so. Besides, Hunchag's creed and course was not encouraged or approved by the Armenians themselves. There was among the Armenians a common suspicion that either Russia had intentionally prepared and sent them in order to arouse disturbances and create a chance to carry her selfish purpose, or that these persons were only hired agents of the Turkish Government to excite the Moslem population. Learning these things, how could the Armenians show sympathy for such a movement? Suppose that these few Russian Armenians were conspirators and murderers, could this justify the government for the universal massacres of the thousands of innocent Armenians, men, women and children? Who could justify the Spanish Government had she undertaken to plunder and massacre all the Italians in Spain for the murder of Canovas by an Italian anarchist? Who could blame Americans that John Wilkes Booth shot President Lincoln? Another fact is, that the greatest devastation and slaughter has been made in places where the Armenian people had no information of or sympathy with the Hunchag movement, and were most submissive to the local government. Besides, these endless atrocities and the plan of massacres were at work long before the existence of Hunchag. Socialism, anarchism and nihilism are new words and strange ideas for a peaceful, industrious and religious nation like the Armenians. What they demanded from their own government and from the European Powers was safety of life, regard of honor and protection of property and religious liberty—the points which were promised in the schemes of reforms and guaranteed by the Christian governments.

CHAPTER XXVII.

1. **The Massacre of Sassoun, (1894), the First in the Series.** Sassoun is a small, mountainous district in the Province of Bitlis, in the heart of Armenia. The inhabitants of this district, being impoverished by heavy taxes imposed upon them by the Turkish Government and by several tribes of the Kurds, and being oppressed by tortures and outrageous barbarities of these tax-gatherers, were obliged to raise their voices and implore the help of the local and central government. These appeals were responded to by severe Kurdish assaults and increased Turkish atrocities. The Armenians of that district, therefore, decided to oppose the Kurds when they came to collect taxes, upon which the barbarous race, being enraged, made a stronger attack for the purpose of murder and revenge. Among the Kurds whom the Armenians of Sassoun opposed, there were a few Hamidieh Kurdish soldiers, the authorized brigands of Kurdistan, several of whom were killed in the struggle. The exaggerated report sent by the Governor of Bitlis made the Sultan enraged, and accordingly he ordered "the suppression of this Armenian rebellion with the severest means." This was the opportunity which the Sultan was anxiously watching for many years, and for which end he was planning.

198

Thus he ordered his troops to march to the Sassoun district and help the Kurds in their bloody work. This plan being hidden from the Armenians, and most probably from the European Powers, was carried on in a very systematic way. The various Kurdish tribes had received special invitation to take part in this great expedition, and the chiefs, with their men, arrived one after the other, and the total number of the Kurds who took part in the campaign was estimated at 30,000. The Armenians believed in the beginning that they had to do only with the Kurds, but they soon realized that a Turkish regular army, with provisions, rifles and cannons, was standing at the back of the Kurds. Sassoun was doomed whether she submitted or opposed. After two weeks' self-protection against the Kurds they saw that the regular army entered into active campaign. Mountain pieces began to thunder, and the Armenians, having nearly exhausted their ammunition, took to flight, when the Kurds and the Turks pursued them and ruthlessly massacred men, women and children (not less than 10,000), plundered the properties and burned seventy villages, and after many horrible outrages, carried many girls and women to Kurdish and Turkish harems. These things took place in August and September of 1894.

2: **The Scheme of Reforms in The American Provinces.** The news of the Sassoun massacre was concealed about four months, during which time the Turkish Government worked steadily to remove every sign and trace of these hellish deeds. But through

the reports of the American missionaries and the
European consuls and the impartial investigators,
both from England and America, and even the
information from the Turks and Kurds themselves,
the awful news proved to be true, and public
opinion was so aroused in England that the representatives of the Great Powers came together and
prepared a scheme of reforms for the six provinces
where the Armenians were greater in number, namely,
Erzeroom, Van, Bitlis, Diarbekir, Harpoot and
Sivas.

These reforms, which were mild and in the line of
what the Turkish Government had frequently promised,
and the execution of which was entrusted to the
Sultan, involved civil offices, judgeships and public
appointments of Moslems and non-Moslems in the
six provinces proportionately. This, however, while
simple justice, was a bitter pill to the Mohamctans,
who had ruled over the Christians with a rod of iron
for five hundred years. The scheme was presented
to the Sultan on May 11, 1895, but he obstinately
refused to accept them. Spring and summer passed,
the anniversary of the Sassoun massacre arrived, no
redress had been secured, nor the punishment of a
single official, while the greatest butchers were deco-
rated by the Sultan. On the 30th day of September,
some Armenians being indignant of this delay, which
would mean the sleep of death for their race, made a
demonstration to present a petition to the Grand
Vizier in an orderly way, which led to a riot in Constantinople, and several hundred Armenians were

brutally killed. The number of victims in two massacres in Constantinople is estimated at 6,000, mostly laboring men. On the 8th day of October the massacre at Trebizond occurred and about 1,000 were killed. These two unjust massacres obliged the diplomats to insist upon their demands of the signing of the "Scheme of Reforms," which the Sultan did October 16, 1895.

3. Subsequent Massacres. October 16th was a day of rejoicing in Constantinople and in the provinces, but it will be remembered as one of the blackest days in Armenian history. On that day the Sultan professed to accept the Scheme of Reforms, but what he really did, as subsequent events show beyond any doubt, was to sign the death-warrant of the Armenian nation. From this time on reform by massacre was the order of the day. About thirty-five large cities, with hundreds of villages, were given over to slaughter and spoliation, so that by a moderate estimate 100,000 Armenians, the most influential men, were massacred, a greater part of their property was lost, and business ruined. About 40,000 houses and shops, churches and schools were burned. Thousands were forced to accept Islam. Thousands of virgins and pure women, after beastly violation, were captured and carried to the Mohametan harems. About sixty Gregorian and fifteen Protestant and several Catholic ministers were most cruelly martyred, many churches were turned to mosques or stables, the holy utensils and scriptures defiled, and before the altars the most brutal outrages were committed. Many

orphans were taken far away to Turkish houses to be trained in the Mohametan faith. About a quarter of a million widows and orphans and helpless aged people were left to the mercy of nature and their Moslem neighbors. The unspeakable Turk, with a single blow, made the ridiculous scheme of reforms inoperative by reducing the proportion of the Armenians in the mentioned six provinces and in the greater part of the Province of Aleppo, where Zeitoon, being the neuclus, the Silesian Armenians were expecting their share in the promised reform.

The following are the names of 105 Armenian clergymen killed in massacres:

"A. OF THE GREGORIAN ARMENIAN CHURCH.

I.

" PROVINCE OF TREBIZOND.

1–6. Six priests, names not given.

II.

" PROVINCE OF ERZEROUM.

7. Der Kerekine, of Erzeroum.
8. Der Yeghia, of Tevnik.
9. Priest, of Kak.
10. Priest, of Oumdoun.
11. Abbot Timotheus, of Hassan-Kaleh.
12. Archimandrite Khorene Guroyan, of Baibourt.
13. Der Ohannes, of Ksanta.
14. Der Harutiun, of Ksanta.
15. Der Magar, of Plour.
16. Der Krikor, of Bushdi.
17. Priest, of Balakhor.
18. Der Khatt, of Hanksdoun.
19. Der Ghevont, of Monastery of the Illuminator.
20. Priest, of Khunzdrig.
21. Priest, of Karatash.
22. Der Hagop, of Large Armundan.
23. Der Krikoriss, of Little Armundan.

III.

" PROVINCE OF VAN.

24–7. Four priests, of the District of Lower Gargar.
28. Priest of Badagantz.
29. Abbot Bedross, of Sourp.

IV.

" PROVINCE OF BITLIS.

30. Priest, of Khoyt.
31. Der Mukhitar, of Khoyt.
32. Priest, of Vanik.
33. Abbot Isaac, of Holy Cross Monastery.
34. Priest, of Broshentz.
35. Abbot, of Monastery of St. Gamaliel.
36–7. Priests of Yeghikiss.
38. Abbot Sarkiss, of Monastery of the Holy Mediator.

V.

" PROVINCE OF SIVAS.

39. Der Vosgui.
40. Der Gronites.
41. Der Asdvadzadour.
42. Der Reteos, of Istanos.
43. Der Yeghia, of the Church of the Holy Savior at
    Shaban-Kara-Hissan.
44. Der Krikor, of Tamzara.
45. Der Kude, of Tamzara.
46. Der Aharon, of Aghvaniss.
47. Priest, of Sis.
48. Priest, of Anarghi.
49. Der Matteos, of Bousseyid.
50. Der Sarkiss, of Gurassin.
51. Der Michail, of Gurassin.
52. Priest, of Armudan.
53. Bishop Isaac, of Derendeh.
54. Priest of Ashodi.
55. Der Arisdakes, of Zilleh.
56. Der Mgurdich, of Zilleh.
57. Der Vassil, of Vezir-Keupru.

VI.

"PROVINCE OF HARPOOT.

58. Archimandrite Ohannes, of Tadem.
59. Der Harutiun, of Hadousi.
60. Der Sarkiss, of Mouri.
61. Der Seth, of Komk.
62. Der Sarkiss, of Khoylou.
63. Der Hagop, of Tadem.
64. Der Aharom, of Tadem.
65. Der Hagop, of Kesserik.
66. Der Khazar, of Morenik.
67. Der Ohannes, of Husseynik.
68. Der Vahram, of Husseynik.
69. Der Nishan, of Miadoun.
70. Archimandrite Krikor Aprahamian.
71. Der Migerdich Shamlian.
72. Der Kegham Shamlian.
73. Der Nerses Baltayan.
74. Der Kurken Yazidjian.
75. Der Tonig Pakhigian.

VII.

"PROVINCE OF DIARBEKIR.

76. Der Harutiun, of Diarbekir.
77. Der Sacristan, of Diarbekir.
78. Priest, of Ali Pounar.
79. Priest, of Arghani.
80. Der Krikor, of Hava.
81. Der Garabed, of Hava.
82. Der Kevork, of Marshmezra.
83. Der Harutiun, of Tzet.
84. Der Nerses, of Khozad.

"NOTES.

No. 8. Der Yeghia, of Tevnik, was killed while presenting a petition to the Government for protection.

No. 29. The Abbot Bedross, of Sourp, had his tongue torn out and limbs cut off one by one. He was then killed " with tortures."

Nos. 33-35. The Abbot Isaac of the Holy Cross, the priest

of Broshentz and the Abbot of St. Gamaliel were impaled in the form of a cross and then burned.

No. 38. The Abbot Sarkiss, of the Monastery of the Holy Mediator, was first blinded.

No. 43. Shot while conducting funeral services.

No. 49. The body of Der Matteos was treated with the grossest indignity.

No. 56. The eyes of Der Mugurdich, of Zilleh, first destroyed.

No. 57. Der Vassil, of Vizir-Keupru, was burned alive.

"B. OF THE EVANGELICAL ARMENIAN CHURCH.

"The following are the names of twenty-one martyred Protestant pastors in Armenia, compiled by a correspondent of the *Independent:*

1. The Rev. Krikor, pastor at Ichme, killed November 6, 1885.
2. The Rev. Krikor Tamzarian.
3. The Rev. Boghos Atlasian, killed November 13.
4. The Rev. Mardiros Siraganian, of Arabkir, killed November 13.
5. The Rev. Garabed Kilijjian, of Sivas, killed November 12.
6. The Rev. Mr. Stepan, of the Anglican Church, at Maf rash, killed November 18.
7. The preacher of a village of Hajin, killed at Marash, November 18.
8. The Rev. Krikor Baghdasarian, retired preacher at Harput, November 18.
9. Retired preacher at Divrik, killed November 8.
10. The Rev. Garabed Hosepian, pastor at Chermuk, November 5.
11. The Rev. Melcon Minasian, pastor at Shepik, November.
12. The Rev. Aboshe Jacob, pastor at Kutterbul, November 6.
13. The Rev. Jurjis Khudherdhaw, Anteshalian, preacher at Kutterbul, November 6.
14. The Rev. Sarkis Narkashjian, pastor at Chunkush, November 14.

15.   The pastor of the church at Severek, November.
16.   The pastor of the chnrch at Adiaman.
17.   The Rev. Hohannes` Hachadorian, pastor at Kilisse, November 7.
18.   The Rev. Hanoosh Melki, pastor at Karabash, near Diarbekir, November 7.
19.   The Rev. Mardiros Terzian, pastor at Keserik, near Harpoot, November.
20.   The Rev. Hagop Abu Hayatian, pastor at Urfa, graduate of Leipzig, December 29.
21.   The Rev. Hannah Sehda, preacher at Sert.
"How many more there are we do not know."

4. Some Touching Events Reported by Missionaries. "The Kurds being not satisfied by massacre, rapine and plunder of the living at that time, disinterred the body of a minister who died before the troubles, and fired into it volleys of bullets and treated it with almost fiendish indignities."

In another place, very far from the above mentioned, "the Turks broke the marble stones of the grave of a wealthy Armenian who died ten years before the massacres, and taking out the bones crushed them into pieces and scattered all around, making diabolic indignities."

"Children were placed in a row, one behind another, and bullets fired through the line to see how many could be dispatched with one bullet." "Infants and small children were piled one on the other, and their heads struck off. In one instance a little boy ran out of the flames, but was caught on a bayonet and thrown back into the flames." Children were held up by their hair, and cut in two, or had their jaws torn apart."

"At Galigozan many young men were tied hand and foot, laid in a row, covered with brush-wood and burned alive. On the last day of August (1894), the anniversary of the Sultan's accession to the throne, the soldiers were especially urged to distinguish themselves, and they made it a day of the greatest slaughter."

"At another village a priest and several leading men were captured, and all but the priest were killed. a chain was put around the priest's neck and pulled until he was choked, after which several bayonets were planted upright, and he was raised in the air and let fall upon them."

"A man who protested against the degradation of his household was taken to a lonely place in the mountains, and buried up to his neck in the ground. He was left there until wolves came and tore his head to pieces. Four bride-grooms were murdered at one time while vainly attempting to protect their brides against a party of Kurds."

"A missionary and a British vice-consul stayed at the house of an Armenian priest for a few hours. After they had left the village Turks seized the priest, skinned him alive, and stuffed his skin with hay, and hung it in the village street as a warning of worse things to come if the Christians dared to complain of persecution and oppression; and many others."

5. That the Last Armenian Massacres were Premeditated, planned and ordered by the Sultan, is evident from the fact that almost all of them took place

in the six provinces where the scheme of reforms were to be practiced, and the manner, the duration, etc., were all alike; for example, in each place Kurds-and Turkish irregulars and the regular soldiers were sent together; in each place the Christians were disarmed by full promise of protection; in each place the massacres and plunder had a certain limit of time; also began and ended with military bugle-sound; in each place the Turks were told they were obeying the Sultan's order; in each place only Armenians suffered, while other Christian people and foreigners were specially protected; in each place the most influential and young men were selected.

These atrocities were composed of murder, plunder, rape, torture, imprisonment and forcing to Islam. It was very evident that local Turkish authorities in each place had a detailed list in their hands as whom they were to plunder, which house to burn after plundering, which persons to be killed and which to be imprisoned. Those who attempted to. protect themselves were horribly dealt with, and those who were destined for death could not find safety even in their Moslem neighbor's houses or in the government houses. Enforcement to Islam was more eagerly practiced in villages and small towns. Rape and outrage was left to the will of the mob; but as a rule the women and children were not sought for murder in the later massacres. Almost all the slaughtered bodies were destroyed by the Turks themselves. Very few aggressors among Mohametans lost their lives, probably not more than 1,000 in all, besides those who were killed in the Zeitoon and Sassoun struggles.

For the sake of truth and humanity it must be said that some influential Turks defended their neighborhood and personal friends, and gave them shelter and provision for days; and some of them dared to express their disgust against this unjustifiable bloodshed. Some of the murderers are reported to have felt "pain in their brains" and suffered much in their imagination if not in their conscience; but the great majority were very much pleased, yet not satisfied, and waiting eagerly for other orders of exterminating "giaours," and cleansing the country from the filthiness of "infidel hogs," and plainly expressed their sorrow that they did not use the first chance as they should.

CHAPTER XXVIII.

1. **The Armenians as a Nation or Church,** have no immediate connection with any ruling power or stately church. The idea of human brotherhood does not yet seem to have very strong grasp in the hearts of men, faintly manifesting its power over the selfish interests. None of the three great churches of Christendom, Greek, Roman Catholic and Anglican, has any special interest in the Armenian church. The Russian church is rather indifferent, while the Greek and Roman churches feel a decided antagonism towards the Armenian church, though calling her "sister church." As to the denominational Protestantism, nothing can be said definitely. Her independence from the State should not place her in a position of utter indifference and heartlessness toward the cry of these bleeding Christians.

2. **England's Attitude Toward the Armenian Massacres.** The only possible explanation of England's inactivity is her selfishness and fear. If we go back towards the beginning of this century we cannot help but see that England in her activity in the Eastern question showed too much selfishness by repeatedly annulling the probable results of Russia's invasions on the soil of "the sick man of Europe,"

and by supporting the "great assassin" of ages in his barbarous course against Christianity and humanity. The Crimean war, and the following British transactions in the East, all resulted from the same selfish and jealous policy. In the last Russo-Turkish war Russia had reached to St. Stefano, only a suburb of Constantinople, and the Russian officers walked in the streets of this historic capital, and it was thought for some time that the Turk, gathering his "bag and baggage," should migrate back towards the interior of Asia Minor. It was under this terror that "the crown-giver of all the kings upon earth, the Sultan," hurried to sign the Treaty of St. Stefano, one of the terms of which was "Russian occupation of Armenia until the promised reforms were practiced." It meant nothing less than the coercion of Turkish-Armenia, and consequent liberation of a long-enslaved Christian people. But England tried and succeeded in annulling this treaty by obliging the European Powers to have a general conference at Berlin, as if to settle the Eastern question, and at the same time having a secret convention (1878) with Turkey (to protect her in case of Russian attack) and getting Cyprus for the security and facility of this bargain. In all these transactions the outward pretext was "the welfare of the Eastern Christians," but in reality the dominating project was selfish interest. Russia was too wise to ignore these intrigues and too cautious to repeat the same follies again. These last two centuries were very remarkable, with the open antagonism between the

"Blind Black Mosgof" and "Heathen Turk," but
Russia has now changed the methods of carrying
forward her policy, and adopted England's way—
outward friendship and inward machination. Therefore, she did not do anything to prevent the late
Turkish atrocities, but even encouraged the Sultan
by petting and caressing him.

3. **The Armenian Relief Work.** Among these
greatest calamities, and blackest transactions, which
have blotted the glory of the nineteenth century for
eternity, the brightest point was the relief movement
seen among the persons and private churches and religious societies, largely in England and in the United
States. As soon as the sad news of devastation and
need reached these countries, the first thought of
good-hearted Christians were directed to a practical
sympathy, and considerable sums provided and sent
to the region of horrors. During the last three years
a total sum of $150,000 was collected and forwarded
through the Red Cross Society and the American
Missionaries in Turkey. Almost every church in the
United States, without denominational distinction,
united in this blessed act of charity. Among the numerous relief agencies, the American Board, the
Armenian Relief Committees in large cities, the
Women's Christian Temperance Union, the Christian
Endeavor Societies, the "Christian Herald," and many
others, are specially praiseworthy. Had it not been
for this timely help, the number of the starved and
the degree of affliction would be far greater.

Besides, it is a great blessing still to some of the widows and orphans of the martyred Christians to be under the shelter and instruction of local and temporary orphanages lately established in various centers of Armenia, and conducted by the American Missionaries and German Sisters.

All the missionaries in Turkey, being perfectly assured of their personal safety, stood firm in their positions. Most of them have written detailed reports, and thus helped the circulation of the sad news in the civilized parts of the world. Many of them did actual work among the stricken families and churches, and some of them rightly deserved the name of "hero" for their deepest sympathy and generous shelter and self-sacrificing help, and unfatigued labors for the sufferers.

Many Armenian refugees found great help on their way to the United States—especially in France and in Switzerland—and on their arrival to this land of liberty they received temporary shelter, aid, sympathy and work almost everywhere from the Christian men and women who unanimously express their desire for "something to be done to save the long-suffering Armenian nation," at the same time almost always excusing themselves for the governmental policy of the United States, as if "Monroe" was greater than Jesus Christ, and his so-called "Doctrine" was more sacred than the principle of Universal Love; and that politics were more essential than the everlasting Kingdom of Heaven.

The temporal benefit of the above-mentioned hu-
manitarian movement was secondary to its spiritual
blessing for those heavily stricken Christians.   The
tearful prayers, the encouraging messages, the life-
giving presence of so many benevolent Christian
brethren and sisters, helped those afflicted people to
carry their burden with more patience and to meet
death with more courage.

The name of Miss Frances Willard will never be
forgotten by the Armenians for her noble deeds
toward the Armenian refugees at Marseilles, France.
An Armenian woman, writing of Miss Willard, said:
"A precious woman of Christ-like heart, has, by her
tender look and touch, made our unbearable sorrows
lighter.   We could not understand her words, nor
could she understand ours, but we understood her
tears, which flowed freely for us."

CHAPTER XXIX.

THE OUTCOME OF THESE MASSACRES.

The late Armenian massacres, far from being a local or temporary and accidental event, have their deeper and wider effects, that touch the universal interests of the world, and especially of the Christian church. We are very anxious to bring the subject before our readers as the subject of their own interest, from the following point of view:

1. **Islam is a Destructive Power.** Admitting some good principles disclosed in the Koran, be it borrowed or original; admitting some past service of the Arabs in acting as birds to carry the seeds of Greek philosophy to other parts of the world; admitting its temporary effect upon the surrounding heathen tribes, in extending the idea of one God (thongh very erroneous compared with the evangelical idea of divinity), yet, as a whole, its influence has been detrimental and injurious to progress and christianity.

Besides, Islam is not a dead power. Under the hypocritic appearance of humanity, and the imitative mockery of civilization of Islam, still lies the same venomous dragon of the early ages—to ruin the vitality of the Christian church; and whenever it finds an opportunity for its deadly work, it is eager and able to act. The great Queen of England may feel herself happy and proud for the millions of her

Mohametan subjects—as a little girl would feel for some pretty small eggs of snakes. May the Lord grant that she may see her mistake before the season of the ripening of iniquity. It is not necessary to be a prophet for the prediction of a near future outbreak of a united Islam against a divided christianity. The Mohametans themselves are conscious that their end is approaching nigh, and that a great and last conflict will occur between themselves and the ''giaour'' powers of the world before Islam is driven to its former source. They say, ''Sham (Damascus as the capital of Islamic regions) was the first, and Sham will also be the last.'' Islam is praying daily for this final conflict.

The unwise policy of Christendom is to give them time and opportunity to carry forward their long-cherished ambition. The Sultan of Turkey has craftiness and advisers enough to devise plots against ''the giaours'' who are trying to seize his alience against the brother nation. In the history of Islam there has been no more proper time to score a victory upon the Christian world. Egypt and other African territories, India and Afghanistan, Persia and Turkey, all Mohametan countries—and all offended by the policy of England—are finding good help in the anti-British union of Russia and France and unwise co-operation of the hot-headed German Emperor, to rise against England and to throw off her yoke; what then? Just what would be the destiny of a lion-keeper when the beast became excited and let loose? This is not a political dream, but a fearful reality, the pains of which is already begun in the "Houses of England."

2. **England's Influence on the Eastern Question is Decreased.** There was a time when the English Ambassador was the highest authority in Constantinople, and the English papers governed the destiny of the Eastern question. Two years ago British warships could enforce the Dardanelles and command before the walls of Bosphorus. The coward "Sovereign of Turkey" was constantly watching the horizon with his field-glasses to see the smoky trace of the "Ingilis" ironclads. The crisis has passed, the British vessels were ordered back from the mouth of the Dardanelles. That was the decisive victory that Russia gained over England, without firing a single gun. Even in the interior the common people, who know nothing about the geography and history of England, began to speak against her as the "Cahbe Ingilis" (Treacherous English), and to jeer at the Queen and her Prime Minister. The present favorite of the country is Russia, once "the Blind Mosgof, the Black Infidel."

In the arena of Eastern question Russia organized the play, Turkey acted, Armenia suffered and England lost. The writer is not of the opinion that it is too late for England, though far more difficult than ever, to rush into the field and save the present and future generations from the calamity which will follow the unnatural union of Turkish Mohametanism and Russian orthodoxism.

The loss of the English Government means the loss of the Anglo-Saxon influence, something far more preferable than the selfish and avaricious policy of the government, or rather of the millionaires, who, having credited treasures to Turkey, do not want to lose their interest, even if it costs the blood of the Armenian, or any other nation. The loss of the Anglo-Saxon influence means the loss of Christian civilization. Russia, with her despotic policy of the Middle Ages, will be too glad to grasp the staff of the church universal and drive the nations back to the dark centuries.

3. **Christianity is Passing a Test.** This is the most delicate and inevitable phase of the question, and worthy to be considered. What have the Christian nations of the world done *to save* those who have suffered because of their Christianity; and what are they going to do to-day to better their condition, which is more dangerous and deplorable now than ever? Experience of the last Greek war encouraged the Turk in his bloodshed and brutality, and discouraged the Christian element of the country, especially the Armenians who, living largely in the interior, have little connection with the surrounding countries. "Well, it is the business of the governments to act," is the answer of Christian people and ministry. If so, then what is the mission of the church? What has been the influence of the Christian church upon the governments?

What can the Armenians think about their powerful and inactive fellow Christians? What can the Armenian ministers tell to their smitten and scattered flock when they inquire about the cause of their long neglect? What would you think if you had fallen into the hands of a wolf, and seen your older and stronger brothers stand by with folded arms and watch your agonies in cold blood?

The financial relief was necessary and exceedingly helpful in its time; but who does not know that the Armenian needs something more and something different? If the little bread given by a few Christians is taken as the full satisfaction in the conscience of Christendom, we are regretfully obliged to disturb the tranquility of that conscience, and solemnly declare before God and men that Armenia needs more than a morsel of bread. What greater need has ever been shown to the Church of Christ to supply? What more sacred cause was ever presented to the spiritual soldiers of the heavenly kingdom to pray and to fight for?

Going one step further, what are the Mohametans thinking about the sincerity of Christian fellowship, and about the essence of Christian religion? Many Turks were heard to cry, even at the moment of their most bloody deeds, "Now! where is your Christos? Let him come and take you out of our hands!" and the helpless victims groaned in their souls and said "My God! why hast Thou forgotten me?" This is something that the enemies of Christianity would gladly grasp and use it against Christianity. This is something that true and zealous Christians, the advocates and protectors of our holy doctrines, must take into consideration, and act according to their responsibility; knowing that God will never do His part if human agents fail in their parts.

4. . **The Most Remarkable Outcome** of these massacres is the manifestation of Christian life in the old Armenian church. Until recent times the majority of the civilized people had a vague idea of this Eastern nation. The last massacres taught the world about the faith and perseverance of that ancient Christian church. During the fiendish and wholesale slaughter of a few months 100,000 strong and noble men gave their lives for the sake of humanity and religion; though they knew perfectly well that by a single repetition of the short Mohametan creed they could be reckoned "Believers," and the law of Koran would protect them from every harm. The majority of the killed were offered the choice of Islam or the sword; even some were urged by their Mohametan friends and neighbors simply to repeat that one word and be saved. But they were not willing to do this. Not a single Gregorian priest among the eighty-four that were killed with most torturous deaths was willing to be an evil example before their flocks, who were waiting to follow his footsteps. Twenty-one Protestant ministers chose a martyr's destiny rather than a Mohametan name, some of them leaving their motherless children behind them. Catholic ministers were dismembered and tortured to death, still clinging to the faith of the cross. A poor, good man was seized by the mob and brought out of his shop upon the street to be

butchered like a sheep. The Turkish neighbors tried to persuade him to accept Islam and be saved. "You are a harmless, meek man; we will take you from the mob if you will only say that you accept Islam, and afterwards you can pursue your Christian life." He asked two minutes to think. It was granted as an exceptional favor. He at once knelt down upon the cold stone to use these two last minutes in communion with his beloved Savior, and then put his head under the bloody axe, saying: "I cannot deny my beloved Jesus." While he was struggling in his blood his wife was killed at home, and four little children were left orphans. The only son of a widow was killed and the headless body was brought home after three days by a few neighboring friends; and, when the mother learned that her son was slain because he would not deny his Lord, she knelt beside him and kissed his blood-stained hand, and said, with flowing tears: "Rather so, my beloved son, than to see you deny our blessed Jesus!" "Blessed are the dead who die in the Lord."

Following is the English translation of an Armenian mother's letter to her son in the United States:

"My Dear Son: Our silence could not be prevented. We live and die clinging to the cross. Thank God for your safety. Read Psalm seventy-nine and know of us. Pray for us."

ARMENIA.

"ARMENIA, O Armènia!
    Will nations heed thy cry,
Or must thou feel the Moslem's steel
    Till all thy people die?

Thy land that once held Eden,
    Where Adam went to dwell,
The savage Turk by fearful work
    Hath made it now a hell.

Where Noah's mighty mountain
    Uplifts its ancient head,
And views a plain piled high with slain,
    Armenia's martyred dead!

Where maidens, Christian maidens,
    Knelt down to fiendish Kurds,
And on the air they breathed a prayer
    We dare not frame in words.

A prayer that even a savage
    Might listen to with pain,
As daughters fair with bosoms bare
    Begged simply to be slain.

To woman's prayer was answered
    A demon's mocking laugh,
And then the knife that ended life
    Seemed kinder far by half.

O chivalry of England!
    Of Europe!   Of the earth!
Your swords should flash, your cannons crash,
    For human right and worth.

Ought Turkish tigers shepherd
    This primal Christian fold,
And boast of crimes unnumbered times,
    Too awful to be told?

Wake, lion-hearted Richard!
    Shake off the clinging sod!
And once again lead Christian men
    Against these foes of God."

INDEX.

INDEX.—Con.

WS - #0293 - 270824 - C0 - 229/152/12 - PB - 9781330270875 - Gloss Lamination